STUDY GUIDE:

THE NOTES OF A WARRIOR

BY
DR. KEVIN L. ZADAI

© Copyright 2019– Dr. Kevin L. Zadai

ISBN: 9781671242852

All rights reserved. This book is protected by the copyright laws of the United States of America. This book may not be copied or reprinted for commercial gain or profit. The use of short quotations or occasional page copying for personal or group study is permitted and encouraged. Permission will be granted upon request. Unless otherwise identified, Scripture quotations are taken from the New King James Version. Copyright © 1982 by Thomas Nelson, Inc. Used by permission. All rights reserved. Scripture quotations marked AMPC are taken from the Amplified® Bible, Classic Edition, Copyright © 1954, 1958, 1962, 1964, 1965, 1987 by The Lockman Foundation. All rights reserved. Used by permission. Scripture quotations marked AMP are taken from the Amplified® Bible, Copyright © 2015 by The Lockman Foundation, La Habra, CA 90631. All rights reserved. Used by permission. Scripture quotations marked NIV are taken from the HOLY BIBLE, NEW INTERNATIONAL VERSION®, Copyright © 1973, 1978, 1984, 2011 International Bible Society. Used by permission of Zondervan. All rights reserved. Scripture quotations marked KJV are taken from the King James Version. Scripture quotations marked NLT are taken from the Holy Bible, New Living Translation, Copyright 1996, 2004, 2015. Used by permission of Tyndale House Publishers, Wheaton, Illinois 60189. All rights reserved. Scripture quotations marked TPT are taken from *The Passion Translation*, Copyright © 2014, 2015, 2016, 2017, www.thepassiontranslation.com. Used by permission of BroadStreet Publishing Group, LLC, Racine, Wisconsin, USA. All rights reserved. All emphasis within Scripture quotations is the author's own. Please note that Dr. Zadai's style capitalizes certain pronouns in Scripture that refer to the Father, Son, and Holy Spirit, and may differ from some publishers' styles. Take note that the name satan and related names are not capitalized. We choose not to acknowledge him, even to the point of violating grammatical rules.

Dedication

I dedicate this book to the Lord Jesus Christ. When I died during surgery and met with Jesus on the other side, He insisted that I return to life on the earth and that I help people with their destinies. Because of Jesus' love and concern for people, the Lord has actually chosen to send a person back from death to help everyone who will receive that help so that his or her destiny and purpose is secure in Him. I want You, Lord, to know that when You come to take me to be with You someday, it is my sincere hope that people remember not me, but the revelation of Jesus Christ that You have revealed through me. I want others to know that I am merely being obedient to Your Heavenly calling and mission, which is to reveal Your plan for the fulfillment of the divine destiny for each of God's children.

Acknowledgments

In addition to sharing my story with everyone through the books *Heavenly Visitation: A Guide to the Supernatural, Days of Heaven on Earth: A Guide to the Days Ahead, A Meeting Place with God, Your Hidden Destiny Revealed, Praying from the Heavenly Realms: Supernatural Secrets to a Lifestyle of Answered Prayer, The Agenda of Angels, Supernatural Finances, Receiving From Heaven, You Can Hear God's Voice,* and *The Mystery of the Power Words,* the Lord gave me the commission to produce this book, *The Notes of a Warrior.* This book addresses some of the revelations concerning the areas that Jesus reviewed and revealed to me through the Word of God and by the Spirit of God during several visitations. I want to thank everyone who has encouraged me, assisted me, and prayed for me during the writing of this work, especially my spiritual parents, Dr. Jesse Duplantis and Dr. Cathy Duplantis. Special thanks to my wonderful wife Kathi for her love and dedication to the Lord and me. Thank you, Sid Roth and staff, for your love of our supernatural Messiah, Jesus. Thank you to a great staff for the wonderful job editing this book. Special thanks, as well, to all my friends who know about *The Notes of a Warrior* and how to operate in this for the next move of God's Spirit!

Contents

Introduction……………………………………………………………...……11

Chapter 1 Facts Vs. Truth……..……………………………………………...13

Chapter 2 The Least is Greater……………………………………………….27

Chapter 3 What You Sow You Reap……………..…………………………..44

Chapter 4 The Origin and Operation of Your Enemy…………………………56

Chapter 5 Know No Limits…………………………………………………….70

Chapter 6 The Middleman……………………………………………………...86

Chapter 7 The Slanderer………………………………………………………..97

Chapter 8 Centurion Faith…..………………………………………………...108

Chapter 9 The Counsel of God……………………………………………….123

Chapter 10 Tied Up or Caught Up……………………………………………134

Introduction

When I was instructed by the Lord to release the message *The Notes of a Warrior*, I was traveling on a plane to preach overseas. The Lord instructed me to change the direction of my teaching's focus for that particular trip to releasing the secret battle strategies of a warrior. I was so surprised that the Lord was allowing me to teach on this new material. I realized, as He unfolded to me His plan of releasing this revelation, that it was the proper season, and much needed at this time. The *"Notes of a Warrior"* study guides are a multi-volume work that will give the reader an intimate view—through the eyes of a warrior—the revelations I have received by the Spirit, through the Word of God. As you walk with Jesus, you'll find Him to be a Victorious Warrior. It is time to experience total victory in your life through Him! The *Notes of a Warrior* will impart understanding to you as we all begin to participate in the next transformative move of our Father, God. Enjoy the *Notes of a Warrior*!

CHAPTER 1

Facts Vs. Truth

"Who Himself bore our sins in His own body on the tree, that we, having died to sins, might live for righteousness—by whose stripes you were healed."
1 Peter 2:24

DISCUSSION:

You are going to need discernment like never before in the days ahead. Not everyone that comes in the name *of the Lord* comes *from the Lord*, and I saw in the Spirit that satan has been tampering with truth; he has been tampering with God's goods. Not everything that is a fact is truth. What is it that is lying to you right now? It may be a fact, but is it the truth? You will see events take place, but it is not the truth because satan can tamper with truth and twist it. You might feel sick tonight, and that may be a fact, but the Bible says, "By His (Jesus') stripes, you are healed" (see Isaiah 53:5). That was true before you were even born because the Lamb was slain before the foundations of the world (see Revelation 13:8), and that is absolute truth from Heaven. Before the universe was lit up, Jesus and the Father were together with the Holy Spirit, and They made a plan. Part of that plan was that someday you would be born, and a book was written about you in Heaven before you ever came to be.

- **Psalm 139:16** "Your eyes saw my substance, being yet unformed. And in Your book they all were written, The days fashioned for me, When *as yet there were* none of them."

  - Please read all of Psalm 139 in the TPT and NKJV versions.

- Some Christians act like there are pages that are missing from their books in Heaven.
- You cannot judge God by your experiences.
- While the Apostle Paul was in jail, he said, "I consider myself a happy man" (see 2 Corinthians 7:4).
- Paul said, "I was appointed as an apostle since birth (see Galatians 1:15)," even though Paul had been killing Christians half of his life.
- Paul said, "I've wronged no man" (see 2 Corinthians 7:2). How could he talk like that? The answer is, he knew the absolute truth, not facts.
- God wants people to be fully convinced about absolute truth. Absolute truth was established before you were born.
- What God proclaimed about you is the absolute truth, and it cannot be revoked.

List some of the absolute truths that your Heavenly Father says about you in His Word.

_____
_____
_____
_____

- ❖ **Romans 11:29** AMP "For the gifts and the calling of God are irrevocable [for He does not withdraw what He has given, nor does He change His mind about those to whom He gives His grace or to whom He sends His call]."

  - The reason it says that the gifts and callings of God are irrevocable is that it is already written. It is too late; it has already been written about you.

- God has a good future written about you; your expected end. There are plans for you to prosper (Jeremiah 29:11). That is the absolute truth.
- Are you going to judge God by the facts or are you going to judge God by His truth and His Word?
- You must be fully convinced, and your faith must rest on only Christ alone.
- This whole country could be turned upside down in a short amount of time; because what this country needs, you have!
- People have forgotten how this country began, and what it was established on.
- One day, people are going to realize that they need to get back to the foundation (see 1 Corinthians 3:11) (see Matthew 7:24-25).

With the Holy Spirit's help, write down any fact that is lying to you right now about your life. Repent and choose to believe the truth of God.

_____
_____
_____
_____

GOING TO THE OTHER SIDE

- ❖ <u>**Mark 4:35-36**</u> "On the same day, when evening had come, He said to them, "Let us cross over to the other side. Now when they had left the multitude, they took Him along in the boat as He was. And other little boats were also with Him."

- After speaking to the people all day, Jesus went down to the lake and told the disciples to get in the boat.
- Jesus said, "Let us go to the other side."
- Something about warfare that we do not understand is that before we enter into the battle, we establish the boundaries.
- **<u>Warrior Note</u>: The first secret of a warrior. You establish your boundaries *before* you go to war. You do not create boundaries when things are coming at you. You do not make decisions based on trauma and emergencies.**
- You make them in the war room before you actually go to war. You establish the truth; you establish objectives.
- War can only be fun if you win, but you create it beforehand. You do not send people to war and say, "I hope it goes well."
- There is planning; there is the establishment of truth and boundaries.

❖ Jesus did not say that they were going to *try* to go to the other side. He said *we are going* to the other side; let us *go* to the other side. That is absolute truth.

- Do you want to know why? Because Jesus did nothing unless His Father told Him to do it.
- It was as though Jesus had His little earpiece in, and He got a message from the Father from the war room, "Jesus, go to the other side."
- Jesus told me that He had visions all the time while He was on earth. Jesus also had discernment while He walked on this earth.
- You need to also have discernment because not everything that is told to you is the truth.
- God is not mocked, and a man will reap what he sows. Are the circumstances in your life mocking God? *He is not going to have it.*
- God is going to come in, and He is going to correct it for you. Do you have faith? Do you have a Father in Heaven who loves you?

- Do you know that Jesus Christ has established direct communication with you? Heaven is hooked up to your frequency; He is talking right now. Heaven, the war room, is calling, **"Go to the other side."**

❖ Jesus heard from the Father and saw visions. Just like when you get flashes sometimes when you are praying or when you are asleep. You are getting peeks into the other realm.

- In Heaven, there is no time or distance like we have down here.
- There are no limits put on you in the Heavenly realm. The limits are here on this earth.
- You live in two realms as a Christian; you are a spiritual being in an earthly body.
- You are born again of the Spirit of God, and a new creature in Christ. "Old things have passed away and behold; all things are now new" (see 2 Corinthians 5:17).
- You are in a body, but your body is limited. However, the Spirit of God inside of you has never doubted you and is not limited.
- **<u>Warrior Note:</u> You are establishing one of the boundaries for warfare. You are being sent, *"not went"*, and God is not steering you wrong. You found yourself in the exact place that God has for you.**
- You must remember this because you are going to need it when you go to war.

As a Christian, you must learn to operate in two realms. What are the two realms? How do you learn to navigate them both?

_____
_____
_____
_____

- ❖ **Mark 4:37-38** "And a great windstorm arose, and the waves beat into the boat, so that it was already filling. But He was in the stern, asleep on a pillow. And they awoke Him and said to Him, "Teacher, do You not care that we are perishing?"

  - Jesus gets in the boat to go to the other side, and halfway across a storm comes.
  - I asked Jesus, "Why were you asleep in the boat." He said, "Because I am going to the other side; I am not dying."
  - Jesus could sleep because He knew that He was not going to sink!
  - Jesus does not tell you to do something and then sits on His throne and gets nervous.
  - Jesus told you to go to the other side; you were sent.
  - **Warrior Note: You do not do anything until God has made it clear what He has established for you to do.**
  - That is absolute truth from the throne.

- ❖ **Mark 4:39-40** "Then He arose and rebuked the wind, and said to the sea, "Peace, be still!" And the wind ceased and there was a great calm. But He said to them, "Why are you so fearful? How *is it* that you have no faith?"

  - The disciples were so fearful that they had to wake Jesus.
  - Knowing that this was satan trying to stop what the Father had told Jesus to do, He got up, and rebuked the wind and the waves. He told the wind and sea to literally "shut up."

DISCUSSION:

The same words that Jesus used here to rebuke the wind and waves on the Sea of Galilee are the same words God used to rebuke Moses and the Israelites at the Red Sea (see Exodus 14:15). The people were crying out, and Moses went and cried out to God and said, "You know you sent us out here to die; we are down here at sea, and Pharaoh's army is behind us, and the people started to cry out." God had already delivered them, and they were already well on their way because the Word of the Lord had come, and Moses was leading them out. When Moses went to God, he was in a war, but he had let the war get into him. The Israelites were in a battle, but the fight got into Moses because the people pressured him, and that was when he started crying out to God. The first thing that God said was, "Shut up," and tell the people to "Shut up." God asked Moses, "What is in your hand?" It was the same tool that got them out of Egypt; it was his staff. Moses took his staff and went down to the water and it parted. We see the same thing happening again with Jesus on the Sea of Galilee. Jesus was telling the storm to "Shut up."

- ❖ **2 Corinthians 10:4-5** "For the weapons of our warfare *are* not carnal but mighty in God for pulling down strongholds, casting down arguments and every high thing that exalts itself against the knowledge of God, bringing every thought into captivity to the obedience of Christ,"

    - Anything that sets itself up against what God has already proclaimed, exalts itself above the knowledge of God.
    - Look at what happened; The sea was in the way of Moses and the people, and it had to split.
    - Jesus rebuked the waves because the storm had set itself against God's Word. The waves became calm, and Jesus along with the disciples got to the other side.
    - We find that on the other side, there was a man waiting for Him that was possessed with a legion of demons (see Mark 5:9).
    - That man was the territorial head of the area that sent the storm, and Jesus was going into war.
    - **Warrior Note: So, why are you surprised when God sends you into a war and a storm comes? Why are you surprised?**

- You see, the storm was not the war. The war was on the other side, and that was where Jesus needed to go. He needed to take out that territorial spirit.

Write down a time when you were in battle with something in your life that exalted itself against the knowledge of God. What spiritual truths did you apply to overcome it?

_____
_____
_____
_____

❖ When Jesus got out of the boat on the other side, He was ready. Are you ready? You are going to have to address the territorial spirit of where you live.

- If you are going to do anything for God, you are going to have to be sent.
- Systems are corrupt. Even the banking system is corrupt, and you have been sent to disrupt those systems by bringing the Kingdom of God.
- You operate in another kingdom where everything is the Lord's, and you must live like that. You must take the emergency brake off.
- The Kingdom of God needs people who are going to side with what God is doing on this earth.
- It's time to take back everything that the devil stole from mankind. And you do that by going to the other side.
- When you get there, you should not act surprised if there is a man full of demons trying to talk to you.

- God trusts you, and that is why he sent you across. He did not send you to cry, "Why does this always happen to me?" Do not do that.
- God needs one person that will go after the devil and not sit and hide.

❖ When Jesus went to the other side and got out of the boat, He immediately met a man who was possessed by many demons (see Mark 5:1-13).

- The devil knowing who Jesus was, knew that he would have to go out of the man.
- The demons started to negotiate with Jesus and asked Him to not send them out of the area when Jesus was casting them out.
- The demons wanted to stay around that region and implored God not to torment them before their time.
- The legion of demons begged Jesus to send them into the herd of pigs on the hillside nearby.
- Jesus knew that those pigs were used as a sacrifice in the temple to Zeus.
- Jesus killed two birds with one stone when He cast them into the pigs, and they ran off the cliff.
- Satan was already negotiating with Jesus the Son of God on how far He was going to send him out.
- Do you know that those demons are on commission? They get credit for all the deeds that they cause to happen, and they report back.
- Those demons were assigned to make sure that there were sacrifices made to pagan gods.
- They thought that they could still get credit for sacrificing a pig, so they asked Jesus to send them into the pigs.
- **Warrior Note: You know that you have overcome the enemy when he starts negotiating his exit!**

- ❖ satan desires to have you (see Luke 22:31), but he cannot, so what are you going to do to damage him?

  - Who is going to be the one to stand up to the enemy who has already been made a show of openly, and was triumphed over through the cross of Jesus Christ (see Colossians 2:15)?
  - Are you going to get over being afraid to die? Once you get over that, you will really live.
  - What was the first thing that happened after Jesus raised Lazarus from the dead? The Pharisees conspired to kill him because they wanted to get rid of the evidence.
  - When Jesus was sacrificed, many people got raised from the dead and wandered throughout Jerusalem. What do you think they did with all those people?
  - They all returned to their homes. Everyone knew that there had been a funeral for them, and now they were alive!
  - After Jesus was raised from the dead, He preached the Kingdom of God. It was a 40-day seminar on the Kingdom, and no one stopped Him.

Jesus has already openly triumphed over the enemy through the cross. What can you do to take down satan in your area of influence?

_____
_____
_____
_____

BE TRANSFORMED

- ❖ <u>**Romans 12:2**</u> "And be not conformed to this world: but be ye transformed by the renewing of your mind, that ye may prove what is that good, and acceptable, and perfect, will of God."

- Transformation is why Jesus died. When Jesus sent me back, it was to make disciples of all nations.
- I want people to be permanently changed and transformed. Are you ready to be transformed?
- This means that no matter what face the devil makes at you—no matter what he says—you tell him he must go.
- You keep driving the devil out, and never let him rest. Never allow him to have an advantage over anything.
- The system of this world is corrupt. The only way to make it through is to have the incorruptible seed within you.

❖ **Jesus is the incorruptible seed, it is the Word of God, and it is in you.**

- Jesus transforms you, and you become that incorruptible seed.
- This seed is something that you eat; it is bread from Heaven. It is the Lord Jesus Christ, and He has offered Himself. When you eat of Him, you are changed. This is transformation.
- I did not come back to this broken world to make you feel good. If I speak the truth in love and you adopt it, it becomes part of you. And when it truly becomes part of you, that's when you begin to feel good!
- I am not your doctor. There is only one hero in Heaven, and it is not me. The last time I checked, you are not on the list either.
- There is one person who is the hero, and He bought it all back for us. It is Jesus, our Savior.
- Jesus sits in Heaven and laughs at your enemies because they are coming to nothing.

What is the "incorruptible seed? How do you obtain it? What does it do?

_____
_____
_____

❖ What happens if you get over the fear of death and you keep living? What happens is nothing that satan throws at you bothers you anymore.

- That's when you have become like the Son who was sent to not only redeem you but to teach you how to walk in two realms.
- Jesus was a Master of two realms. He could walk in the Spirit, and He could walk in the flesh. He had command about Him, and He wasn't afraid to offend people.
- He offended people everywhere He went, except those who loved Him and adhered to His sayings.

John 1:12 KJV "But as many as received Him, to them gave He power to become the sons of God, even to those that believe on His name:"

- To those people who love and adhere to Jesus, He gave authority and power.
- The word "power" used here is the word *exousia* in Greek.
- You might think of the raw power of an explosion, but it is better than that.
- You do not need to have a certain natural stature to have authority.
- **You just have to know who you are.**
- It does not matter how much you weigh or how much you can bench press.
- It does not even matter how big your gun is. What matters is, *do you know who you are?*
- Jesus addressed that devil on the other side, and He cast a legion of demons out of the possessed man (see Luke 8:26-35). When Jesus did that, it broke the power of the devil over that whole region.
- That possessed man had turned that entire area upside down and was terrorizing everyone. Jesus had to take out the head which was the territorial spirit living in that man.

- I am here to tell you that your relationship with God is going to cause confrontation, and you cannot avoid it.

❖ How convinced are you that you are a sent one? As I said before, the system down here is corrupt. And if you walk into any situation praying in the Spirit, full of the Word of God, something is going to change, and it is not going to be you. It is going to be everything around you.

- You are a sent one!
- I am not talking about just the Five-Fold ministry of the church.
- There is a legitimate Five-Fold ministry (see Ephesians 4:11-13).
- The Apostle Paul labels the Five-Fold as apostle, prophet, pastor, teacher, and evangelist and says that *God sets them* in the church.
- The Word of God says that God sets them in the church, *not us*.
- You cannot appoint yourself as an apostle *only God can*.
- Then there are gifts of the Spirit.
- Paul said that these are given as the *Spirit* wills, and *not* as you will (see 1 Corinthians 12:11).

❖ **The Lord Jesus pointed out to me how everybody is labeling themselves as apostolic or prophetic now, and He told me it all has to do with accountability. I saw that what is missing today is that no one wants to be held accountable. In the Old Testament, if you missed it as a prophet, you were stoned to death.**

❖ **Paul talked about being a good soldier of Christ. You need to allow the incorruptible seed, the Word of God, to mature you to the point where you can propagate the gospel into other people's lives. You will begin to influence people like Paul did.**

Explain how you can be transformed as a born-again believer?

_____
_____
_____
_____

CHAPTER 2

The Least Is Greater

"As they departed, Jesus began to say to the multitudes concerning John: 'What did you go out into the wilderness to see? A reed shaken by the wind? But what did you go out to see? A man clothed in soft garments? Indeed, those who wear soft clothing are in kings' houses. But what did you go out to see? A prophet? Yes, I say to you, and more than a prophet. For this is he of whom it is written:' 'Behold, I send My messenger before Your face, who will prepare Your way before You.' "Matthew 11:7-10

DISCUSSION:

Jesus asked the multitudes concerning John the Baptist, "What did you go into the wilderness to see? A reed shaken by the wind?" The answer to this is "No," because John was more than a prophet. He was a messenger of God sent to prepare the way. John would look at you and say, "Repent." Do you know that he would not even get on Christian TV today? John the Baptist's sermon was six seconds, but to be on TV, you must have at least 30 minutes. His six seconds included "Repent for the Kingdom of God is at hand." Don't you have anything else? Do you have a book? Do you have any other sermons? "No." He would not be on a Christian TV show today. How many miracles have you had? "None." Have you had anybody raised from the dead? "No." Any healings? "No." Any demons cast out? "No."

- ❖ <u>**Warrior Note**</u>**: I am giving you another secret of a warrior here. "He who is least in the Kingdom of God is greater than John the Baptist."**

  - Jesus brought up John in front of everyone, and He said, "Assuredly, I say to you, among those born of women there has not risen one greater than John the Baptist; but he who is least in the Kingdom of Heaven is greater than he" (see Matthew 11:11).
  - News flash: From now on, the least—the littlest one in the body of Christ—is greater than John the Baptist.
  - Be very careful; that Christian who you like to make fun of? Well, you better watch it because John the Baptist wants to meet *him*.
  - You call that Christian weak, but he or she is above John the Baptist because of the New Covenant.

Why is the least in the Kingdom of God now greater than John the Baptist, according to the New Covenant?

_____
_____
_____
_____

WARFARE

- ❖ When you go into warfare, you already know what side you are on. And you know that everyone else is going to fall on their side, whatever side that is.

  - Why are you surprised when it gets confusing, and things start to turn into a whirlwind?
  - Congratulations! You have just entered the war zone.
  - <u>**Warrior Note:**</u> **In the war zone, you have to know what you believe, and you must have a command about you.**

❖ Everything was fine for me, but then God asked me to go to Puerto Rico and teach them how to take out hurricanes and poverty!

- If it is the Gospel, it has to work everywhere.
- I could be in my three-piece suit, staying in the most beautiful hotels and preaching on prosperity, but it had better work in a third world country in shorts and a ball cap.
- God made me go to Puerto Rico and teach on how to take out hurricanes, and how to take your authority in the Spirit.
- There were about 17 people in that congregation and on this particular trip, I preached on prosperity in 14 different sessions.
- I taught them that God wants you to prosper so that you can do His work on the earth.
- I taught them to exercise authority over their body daily, and to say I am healed.
- I taught them how to partake of the Scriptures, and I how to confront the enemy.

❖ **John 10:10** "The thief cometh not, but for to steal, and to kill, and to destroy: I am come that they might have life, and that they might have it more abundantly."

- Jesus said. The thief has come to steal, kill, and destroy. What do you not understand about your enemy?
- What Jesus is saying here is that if anybody comes into your life and is killing, stealing, or destroying, that is the thief; that is your enemy satan.
- Then Jesus tells you that He has come to give you life. Not only life but life more abundantly. He said, "The words that I speak to you are Spirit, and they are life" (John 6:63). We are not wrestling against flesh and blood (see Ephesians 6:12).

- Once you bind these devils, and you drive them out, the people you are praying for start to act right. Once you drive the enemy out, people are free (see John 8:36).
- When Jesus went to the other side and cast the devil out of that man, the man put his clothes on and was in his right mind. That was because the enemy was driven out.
- What is it that is bothering you? Whatever is coming against you is your assignment to take out!

❖ **Warrior Note: This is another secret. Whatever it is that you are dealing with: That is your assignment.**

- David ran at Goliath and told the giant that he was going to feed him to the birds that day. David said that when he was finished with Goliath that he was going to take off his head (1 Samuel 17:44-46).
- David said that Goliath was an uncircumcised Philistine and that he lacked covenant. Circumcision was a covenant. He asked Goliath how he dared to come against and defy the armies of the Living God?
- **That is what you must do: You must wake up every morning and tell the devil what you are going to do to him today!**
- Jesus did this every morning. Jesus said that He had been sent to do the will of the Father. He came to give life and life more abundantly (see John 10:10). He came to heal the sick, drive out devils, raise the dead, and preach the Good News. Jesus said He came to proclaim the year of Jubilee and to break yokes (see Luke 4:18-19). And every day, He went out, and that is what He did.
- I am not playing games, and you should be the same way.
- Come out swinging every morning asking the devil how dare he try to defy you and your family!

THE NOTES OF A WARRIOR

How has the devil been defying you in your life? Take the time now to pray, bind him, and drive him out.

_____
_____
_____
_____

- ❖ This is what I am going to do today. I am going to invest my money, and it is going to prosper. I am going to lay hands on the sick, and they are going to be healed. I am going to drive out devils. I am going to speak a Word of deliverance to many people. I have said that since I was 19 years old.

  - I have a Word in my mouth. It is a Word of deliverance for many people.
  - When I got saved, I was called out by an evangelist, and by the power of the Holy Spirit, he said over me, "Thou shalt speak a word of deliverance to many people, thus saith God." That was in 1980.
  - Now I see that God has put me everywhere, and I am not backing off.
  - If I am not backing off, don't you want to stay in there too? Do not back off.
  - As soon as people start saying, "Hey, can you tone it down a little bit?" I start cranking it up, and I do not even let them finish. Why? Because I now know—I know I got him—I got the devil!
  - **When he starts negotiating a position, you know you got him.**
  - Somebody has got to be bold. Somebody has got to stand up and say, "It cannot stay the way it's been."
  - Christianity is not a feel-good religion

- ❖ **Christianity is transforming because it creates disciples.**

  - When you had a mentor, a rabbi, or a teacher, they would have their students follow their disciplines.

- It was common to have teachers walking around with disciples. They were adhering to the disciplines of their teacher—their rabbi.
- That was how they became known as disciples. They adhered to the disciplines of their teacher.
- When we mention discipline, everybody kind of steps back, but God loves those He disciplines.
- God is calling you a son and a daughter when He disciplines you (see Hebrews 12:6 AMP).
- I know some elite soldiers, and they are not afraid of death.
- When I died, I went to be with the Lord, and it was a promotion.
- When you die as a Christian, it is a promotion, and there is a celebration in Heaven.
- You are not even told how you died. I did not know how I died until Jesus told me.
- If you know you cannot lose, then while you are living, you might want to start swinging!

❖ **Jesus talked to me about Samson and how he was born to pick a fight.**

- To understand Samson fully, you have to go back to the angel visit that his mother had (see Judges 13:1-24).
- It says that God was looking for a reason to provoke and make war with the Philistines.
- Samson was born to pick a fight.
- **<u>Warrior Note:</u> Do you understand that when Yahweh spoke *your* name, He was picking a fight?**
- **When He spoke you into your mother's womb, He was picking a fight with this generation; with territorial spirits that you were born into in a particular area.**
- *You were born to pick a fight with the devil.*
- Samson would look at the enemy, and he would say, "You are messing with the wrong God. And if the power of God comes on me, I cannot be responsible for what I am about to do."

- The power of God would come on Samson, and he would supernaturally be able to do battle against the Philistines.
- He ripped off their gates, which were the strongest part of the city. He ripped them off and carried them up a mountain (see Judges 16:3).
- He burned their crops. Have you ever tried to catch a fox? Well, try catching two of them and tying their tails together. If you get that far, then put a torch in between that knot. There you have what Samson did (see Judges 15:4-5).
- One day, he had all these Philistines surround him, and he looked down and saw a donkey jawbone. He picked it up and started swinging; when it was over, a thousand soldiers were dead (see Judges 15:16).
- Do we have any warriors reading this Study Guide?

❖ Being neutral *is* taking a position; you have opted *out* of the war. The war is spiritual, and you do not use physical weapons. "The weapons of our warfare are not carnal but mighty through God for pulling down strongholds" (see 2 Corinthians 10:4).

- We have actual footage of when we came against demons and the footage actually shows the effects of it when we pronounce the name of Jesus, and we pray in the Spirit. The demons flee, and we have cameras that catch it.
- I preach and talk about the Son of God and the blood of Jesus. I proclaim the name of Jesus until there are no demons left.
- What happened was someone stood up and proclaimed the Name above all names, Jesus. Someone went to war.
- I want everyone reading this not to be afraid of the devil.
- I want everyone reading this, not to be afraid to die.
- I want everyone reading this not to be afraid to let God live through you so that everyone knows that God is with you!

In what areas of your life have you been afraid to engage in spiritual warfare? Stand up and take your authority in Jesus' name!

_____
_____
_____
_____

FAVOR IS FROM THE LORD

- **Deuteronomy 28:1-2** "Now it shall come to pass, if you diligently obey the voice of the LORD your God, to observe carefully all His commandments which I command you today, that the LORD your God will set you high above all nations of the earth. And all these blessings shall come upon you and overtake you, because you obey the voice of the LORD your God:"

- **Deuteronomy 28:12-13** "The LORD will open to you His good treasure, the heavens, to give the rain to your land in its season, and to bless all the work of your hand. You shall lend to many nations, but you shall not borrow. And the LORD will make you the head and not the tail; you shall be above only, and not be beneath, if you heed the commandments of the LORD your God, which I command you today, and are careful to observe *them.*"

- **Deuteronomy 15:4** "except when there may be no poor among you; for the LORD will greatly bless you in the land which the LORD your God is giving you to possess *as* an inheritance."

  - Favor is not fair. You cannot be afraid of favor; it is from the Lord.
  - I saw that favor was written in my book before I was born.
  - In the book of Revelation, it says that God will give you a white stone, and it has your new name on it, which has always been your name (see Revelation 2:17).

- Victory is my name. Why? The devil tried to kill me, and he could not because my name is Victory. Do you understand that it is connected to my destiny?
- You need to find out what God calls you.

❖ I was in your future. Everything is going to work out fine. I saw all of us at the end of the age, giving the Lamb what He deserves, *all* of our praise.

- Jesus was getting His reward for His suffering.
- So many white-robed people from all the ages were worshipping the Lamb, and Jesus was basking in it. This is what I saw.
- I saw angels falling before Him.
- What about a heartfelt passion that drives us to encounter the Holy One?
- What about a real encounter with the Holy Spirit that causes us to change?
- How about a transformation that is so profound that the devil sees that another one has hooked up with the Holy One? Another child of God has hooked up with their destiny.
- God sent Jesus to blaze a path that has now become an eight-lane highway for us.

❖ **Isaiah 35:8-10** "A highway shall be there, and a road, and it shall be called the Highway of Holiness. The unclean shall not pass over it, but it *shall be* for others. Whoever walks the road, although a fool, shall not go astray. No lion shall be there, nor shall *any* ravenous beast go up on it; It shall not be found there. But the redeemed shall walk *there,* and the ransomed of the LORD shall return, and come to Zion with singing, with everlasting joy on their heads. They shall obtain joy and gladness, and sorrow and sighing shall flee away."

- There is a highway of holiness. This highway is established as holy, that if a fool accidentally finds himself on it, he will cease to be a fool.
- Now that is a transformation! That is the Jesus I met that sent me back to you.
- I am telling you; you have got to have an edge about you from the other realm. You have got to be touched from the other realm.
- The Holy One, the Holy Spirit has been sent, to teach you, to lead you, to guide you, to transform you, so that you have a command about you so that when you get into the boat, you go to the other side.
- When you get there, you drive out devils, and you free a whole city, and this is the Gospel of Jesus Christ.
- Everywhere Jesus went, He proclaimed Jubilee, and that your yokes were broken. He declared that you are free of demons.
- If you accidentally died, you were resurrected.
- Jesus is the resurrection and the life (see John 11:25-26).
- He rose people from the dead. He yanked them out of death's grip.
- He provoked the Jewish leaders to jealousy.
- Have you done that yet? Do you provoke people to jealousy?
- I want to know that you can make a difference in this generation.

How can you provoke others to jealousy for the sake of the Gospel?
_____
_____
_____
_____

❖ I saw that if I do not speak, this generation will hand off the baton to another generation that will not be in a good position because people today are not doing their job.

- During a relay race, every person on their leg of the race must perform at their best. To set records, every person must do their part.

- When the previous generation handed me the baton, I had to have a miracle because I was behind to where mathematically I could not catch up, but I did. I remember feeling the power of God.
- I realized that I could not allow this generation to pass away without encountering the living God in the fullness of what God has for us.
- It is going to be so bright at the end of this age that people will be getting healed on the streets.
- They will be getting into services just so that they can be healed, without anyone touching them. I saw this for the future.
- People in the future may have to wait for two or three services to get into the building where everyone is being healed. The power of God is already here and never left.
- I am here to inform you that you must engage God.

❖ **I am speaking to this generation, and you also must speak to this generation. You have a voice, and it is your location. When you speak, it locates you, and you must speak from where you are. Who you are and what God has put in you are so crucial for this generation. The Body of Christ must rise. You must accomplish what you have been called to do. You cannot focus on facts; you have to focus on absolute truth.**

❖ <u>Isaiah 55:11</u> "So shall My word be that goes forth from My mouth; It shall not return to Me void, but it shall accomplish what I please, and it shall prosper in the thing for which I sent it."

TOUCHED BY THE OTHER REALM

The Lord has never *tried* anything. When I was in Heaven, I was not allowed to use the word *tried*. The word *try* is not in God's vocabulary. When God thinks of what He wants, He speaks it out, and it goes forth with the intent that God has for that Word. God's Word comes back to Him finished, not void. God accomplishes the Word He speaks. He sent His Word and healed them. With a Word, people were healed. With a Word, demons left. Angels are waiting for you to catch on fire so that you start to engage them in your assignment. God's angels do not take no for an answer. Angels are not here to brush your hair and whisper encouragement in your ears. They are military, and all they care about are the directives that they have been sent to perform, and that is the Word of God. They harken unto the voice of the Lord (see Psalm 103:20 KJV), and they do *His* bidding, not yours. I apologize for people all over the world who claim to encounter angels because I know they have not. When you encounter an angel, you do not stay the same. You will pray that you never have another encounter. Every time I have had an angel encounter, I pray I never do again because it is hard on many things. It destroys pride; it is tough on your body. You cannot walk around like a peacock anymore, strutting around because you are not all that. You do not know that until you are knocked on the ground because an angel showed up, and he did not even touch you. This angel was in the presence of your Father; he beheld the face of your Father, and then comes and stands beside you. He wants transformation, and he wants cooperation. He wants somebody that has a command about them.

God has given you a voice for this generation. What is preventing you from speaking forth? What can you do to cooperate more with the Holy Spirit in your life?

_____

_____

_____

_____

- ❖ Isaiah was a major prophet, not a minor one, and he was not a beginner. He was an experienced prophet. Everything was fine until one day, he was caught up to the throne of God, and he saw the Lord Almighty seated, and he became undone (see Isaiah 6:1-5).

    - When was the last time you have been undone?

- The first sign of being undone is when the prophets start to see that they are not prophetic but pathetic. When prophets see that they are pathetic, they become undone, and then they become real prophets.
- Something from the other realm touched Isaiah's lips. It was a live coal from God's holy altar (see Isaiah 6:6).
- Isaiah was fine, and then he became undone. He said, "I am a man of unclean lips, and I dwell in the midst of a people of unclean lips."
- He was touched and spoke from the other realm, and he was healed when the coal touched his lips.
- You need to be touched by that other realm.
- Being born again is not a figment of your imagination.
- You are a son of the Living God, a daughter of the Living God. You have been chosen; you are a chosen generation.
- You are a new creature, and there has never been a species like you (see 2 Corinthians 5:17).
- God has given us the authority to become sons of God. Children of God (see John 1:12).
- We need to be touched by the other realm.

❖ The Holy Spirit came on the day of Pentecost. The Holy Spirit that is inside of you came on the day of Pentecost, and He has not changed. He is the same Holy Spirit that came two thousand years ago (read Acts 2).

- When the Holy Spirit came into the building where they were waiting, there was a mighty wind blowing, with a sound from Heaven.
- The Holy Spirit came with a mighty wind and fire on people's heads.
- The believers then had utterance so that they were speaking in other languages that they did not know.
- People from every nation were in town that day for a feast, and they heard their languages spoken through people that they knew did not speak those languages.
- Peter stood up and apologized to the crowd for his people. He said they were not drunk as some supposed for it was early afternoon.

- This event was to fulfill what was spoken by the prophet Joel in the last days of how God was going to pour out His Spirit on all flesh.

❖ When the Holy Spirit showed up, He showed up with wind and fire, utterance and drunkenness, and look how sophisticated we are today. The Holy Spirit told me that if there is no freedom in a room, then He is not there because where the Spirit of the Lord is, there is freedom (see 2 Corinthians 3:17). He told me that was the test.

- If a person is truly set free, it is because the Son set him free, and he is free indeed, which means he is permanently free (see John 8:36).
- I am done with just having a move of the Spirit for a week and then going back to the same old lifestyle. I am done with that.
- I told the Lord I would come back from the dead, but I want fruit that lasts because that is God's Word.

Describe areas of your life where you have not experienced the freedom of the Spirit that you would like. Take the time now to ask the Holy Spirit permanently set you free.

_____
_____
_____
_____

❖ **John 15:16** "You did not choose Me, but I chose you and appointed you that you should go and bear fruit, and *that* your fruit should remain, that whatever you ask the Father in My name He may give you."

- You will have fruit that lasts, and that sounds permanent. Do you want fruit that is permanent?

- The Holy Spirit that is inside of you has not diminished. He sent me back from the dead to tell people that He is still the same.
- The Commander of your faith, the one who started this, is going to end it, and it is Jesus, the Author, and the Finisher of your faith (see Hebrews 12:2).
- Right now, Jesus is setting you up for a huge breakthrough!
- You have been ordained to live on the earth at this time to work the works of God that were preordained through Christ from the foundation of the world (see Ephesians 2:10).

DOUBT AND UNBELIEF

❖ The books that are written about us in Heaven are so beautiful that no one should go to hell (see Psalm 139:16 TPT). Do you want to know why people are in hell when I saw their books in Heaven? It is because they did not cooperate with God, and they did not believe.

- We are not of those who fall away but of those who obtain the promises (see Hebrews 19:39).
- We do not fall away through doubt and unbelief. Do not be like the children of Israel who fell in the desert because of their unbelief (see Hebrews 3:19).

❖ Everyone who yelled out to Jesus, "Son of David have mercy on me," got healed. The people that knew Jesus from His hometown said, "That is the carpenter's son." They got nothing except a table and chairs.

- Jesus was restricted by their unbelief.
- He could not heal in His hometown except for some minor miracles.
- Unbelief will limit God's will and His work in your life.

- Jesus could not do many miracles in His hometown because they did not discern Him as the Son of David—the Messiah.
- They recognized Jesus as the carpenter's son. That is what they got, somebody that could fix their table and chairs.
- You do not need that. You need an overhaul from Heaven and the hand of the Lord upon you to where you cannot stop prophesying.
- Do not wait until you get to Heaven and look back and wish you had engaged more because that is what I did.
- I looked back and wished that I had engaged more, and Jesus heard it and sent me back, and now I am not going to hold back.
- I am going to preach the Gospel, and the Gospel means Good News.
- It means you do not have to be sick because of what Jesus went through on the cross for you.
- It is time to receive healing from the Lord.
- There are no neutral devils. They have already taken sides, and it is time to drive them out in the authority of the name of Jesus Christ.

❖ **"The Lord says, 'I have drawn My sword and handed it to you; wield My sword, which is My Word, which is able to save your souls; it is the incorruptible seed. Use the sword of the Spirit, the Word of God often. For I surround you like a wall of fire, and I sing songs of deliverance over you because I am a Warrior, and I sing over you. The Lord is a Warrior (see Zephaniah 3:17), and He is fighting.' The Lord says, 'Won't you join in and confirm your victory with Me?' says the Lord." Hallelujah!**

❖ The joy of the Lord is going to break out. The joy is the victory. The Lord is sitting in Heaven and laughing because your enemies have become nothing.

- Do not let the devil draw your attention away but set your mind on things above (see Colossians 3:2) where Christ is seated at the right hand of God with full authority at the throne (see Ephesians 2:6).

- In the Heavenly realms is where you sit with the Lord.
- "Lift up your heads, O you gates! And be lifted up, you everlasting doors! And the King of glory shall come in. Who is this King of glory? The Lord strong and mighty, the Lord mighty in battle" (Psalm 24:7-8).
- The Lord is creating a strong passion in His people to live their lives in obedience, knowing that God cannot fail.
- Engage God, and everything is going to work out just fine.

What is God's assignment for your life? How can you engage with God more regarding your assignment?

_____
_____
_____
_____

CHAPTER 3

What You Sow You Reap

"Do not be deceived, God is not mocked; for whatever a man sows, that he will also reap. For he who sows to his flesh will of the flesh reap corruption, but he who sows to the Spirit will of the Spirit reap everlasting life."
Galatians 6:7-8

DISCUSSION:

If you give and nothing happens, that is not God. I am tired of going to church, and nothing happens. I am tired of Christianity where nothing happens because it is not what Jesus died for. Whatever you put into something; God is going to increase it thousands of times. If you give your life over to Him completely, it will be evident within 24 hours. The problem is that God is being mocked because a man is reaping what he sows and blaming God for it. So, whatever is coming out is what people are putting in. You are never going to stand before Jesus and say it did not work. I was there, and I could not say that because Jesus was so much more. You are not going to blame Him for anything, including inactivity in your life. I come as your friend, and I have been in that situation, and I could not confront or blame Jesus for anything in my life. The only reason that I appeared before Him was that He, in His mercy, allowed me to approach Him. Jesus extended His scepter toward me, and He called me to Himself. He chose me and He had me stand before Him. It is with that reverence that I tell you that everything that comes into this ministry goes into the ministry, including my royalties, which go into Warrior Notes. I believe in what I am doing. However, the reason I give is that I believe in what Jesus sent me back for. Everything that you do for God, you invest in what He is doing in your life. What I am asking you to do is give yourself wholly to Him, and within twenty-four hours, it will begin to explode. "God will not be mocked. A man will reap what he sows" (Galatians 6:7). If you sow towards eternal life, it will start to manifest in every part of your life. Do you understand that I am not going to be a friend if I do not tell you the truth? The truth is that God is mocked because men are reaping what they sow

What is preventing you from giving yourself wholly over to God? How can you begin to sow to eternal life now?

_____
_____
_____
_____

- ❖ **Matthew 15:8-9** "These people draw near to Me with their mouth, and honor Me with *their* lips, but their heart is far from Me. And in vain they worship Me, teaching *as* doctrines the commandments of men."

    - These people are giving God service with their mouths, but their hearts are far from Him because God cannot be mocked.
    - I got to the place where I would rather not be known as a Christian by what I say, but by what happens in my life.
    - Wouldn't you want a divine explosion to happen everywhere you go so that everyone would know that you were a Christian?
    - To know you are a Christian not because of what you said, but the fact that everything shifts in your atmosphere because you have influence with God.

- ❖ There are so many things that can be prevented if you take the time to be sober-minded. Think about what you do and what you say.

- Do you know how many times I was almost killed in an airplane because I trusted someone who said they had done something that they had never done?
- Do you know what it's like to get in the air and find out that people did not keep their word when they worked on the airplane?
- I do not want to be the kind of person that hands-off problems to other people. I consider myself a problem solver.
- I believe in putting myself in a situation where I can meet people's needs by the Spirit of God.
- To meet people's needs by the Spirit of God, you have got to be accountable, which means that God is not going to be mocked.
- Ministers are falling all the time. It is because God is not mocked. A man will reap what he sows. These things do not happen overnight.
- I am not going to hand off the baton to the next generation in an unworthy manner.
- I am going to do my job, and you are going to do your job.

❖ **James 1:21** KJV "Wherefore lay apart all filthiness and superfluity of naughtiness, and receive with meekness the engrafted word, which is able to save your souls."

- Your job is to believe in the One who saved you. To believe in the Father who sent Him. And to accept the engrafted Word in you, which can save your souls.
- The word "soul" here in Greek means "psyche," and it does not mean your spirit.
- Your spirit is saved by the born-again experience, but your *soul* is being transformed and changed by the Word of God (see Romans 12:2).
- You need to be transformed by the renewing of your mind.

WHAT YOU DO NOT KNOW MAY HURT YOU

- ❖ I almost died in a plane crash because of negligence. Even though, as the pilot, I am the ultimate person responsible for the airplane, I depend upon other people to do their job. I have to oversee everything.

    - It is the same way with your spiritual life. The demonic, your enemy, relies on the fact that you either do not know something or that you have misinformation.
    - What you do not know may hurt you, and wrong information that you do have may also hurt you.
    - From now on, your spiritual discernment must go through the roof.
    - Not everything that people say is right, and you need to confirm it.
    - "By the mouth of two or three witnesses every word shall be established" (2 Corinthians 13:1).
    - What matters to me is that someone gets up and yields to the Spirit and speaks by the Spirit, so that people are changed.
    - Change can happen.
    - Transformation is not just for superhuman people.
    - Transformation is for weak people who are about to be made strong by the Spirit of God.
    - The resurrection power of God is able to manifest through weakness.

- ❖ **2 Corinthians 12:9-10** "And He said to me, "My grace is sufficient for you, for My strength is made perfect in weakness." Therefore most gladly I will rather boast in my infirmities, that the power of Christ may rest upon me. Therefore I take pleasure in infirmities, in reproaches, in needs, in persecutions, in distresses, for Christ's sake. For when I am weak, then I am strong."

THE NOTES OF A WARRIOR

What spiritual concepts do you feel the need to have more clarity? List them here and make a plan to ask two or three Christian witnesses.

_____
_____
_____
_____

- ❖ <u>Mark 2:17</u> TPT "But when Jesus overheard their complaint, he said to them, "Who goes to the doctor for a cure? Those who are well or those who are sick? I have not come to call the 'righteous,' but to call those who are sinners and bring them to repentance."

  - Jesus did not come to heal people that were already well.
  - He came to seek those who were lost and to heal the sick.
  - He said that a healthy person does not need a doctor (see Mark 2:17).
  - I want to know the truth even if it hurts.
  - The truth will continue to keep you alive and effective.
  - If you keep God's promises, and if you implement them into your life, they will keep you from being ineffective — His precious promises.
  - His very great and precious promises will cause you to be a partaker of the divine nature (see 2 Peter 1:4).

- ❖ <u>Titus 2:6</u> "Likewise, exhort the young men to be sober-minded,"

  - I have had to work through some emergencies because of other people's negligence.
  - In my Christian walk, I am ultimately responsible for everything, so I have to be sober-minded.
  - Being sober-minded is being aware; being informed.
  - Christians are not weak people.

- Christians may be weak in themselves, but they are strong in the Lord and His mighty power (see Ephesians 6:10).
- Christians are not naive or misinformed (see Philippians 1:9-10).
- Christians should be the most discerning, the smartest and the wisest people on the earth because they walk with God.

❖ **Psalm 112:2-3** "His descendants will be mighty on earth; The generation of the upright will be blessed. Wealth and riches *will be* in his house, and his righteousness endures forever."

- Great and mighty is your offspring on the Earth.
- You have got to know your enemy.
- There are people around you that are misinformed, and they are Christians.
- Misinformed Christians are very dangerous.
- They are like fake news because they spread disinformation.
- They can slant your view based on their agenda, and satan knows how to use them to his advantage.
- You need to become aware of your need for discernment to know how your enemy operates.

Make a list of some of the ways that you can increase your discernment for the days ahead?

_____
_____
_____
_____

- ❖ **2 Corinthians** 5:18-19 "Now all things are of God, who has reconciled us to Himself through Jesus Christ, and has given us the ministry of reconciliation, that is, that God was in Christ reconciling the world to Himself, not imputing their trespasses to them, and has committed to us the word of reconciliation."

THE MINISTRY OF RECONCILIATION

Before I came back from Heaven, I asked Jesus, "How do you explain to a generation their need if they do not see it?" For 30 years, I have worked with some very successful, brilliant, and overqualified people. I had to get them to see their need. I had to present Jesus to them in a way that provides for a need. If I did not provide for a need, then they did not see the relevance of what I was saying. However, if I am partaking of the divine nature, and if I am representing Jesus, not by just word but by a manifestation from the other realm then they want to talk. I was talking to a flight attendant who wanted to know why I was so happy all the time. I said, "Well, you know I died and came back, and every day is a gift to me." She said, "What? Did you die?" I said, "Yeah, I died on the operating table. You didn't know about that?" I told her that everything is written in Heaven as though you are going to Heaven. No one needs to go to hell because Jesus, according to Paul, in 2 Corinthians 5, said that we have the "ministry of reconciliation."

I had to change my world view. I had to change the way I looked at things because people need to have it announced to them that Jesus paid the price. Knowing this causes them to question the false peace and false sense of security that they have. I was with professionals that have all the money they will ever need. They have all the relationships they need, and are satisfied, but they are going to hell. We must present them with something from the other realm that will cause them to question why they have the perception they do. First, I allow the Lord to break down my false perceptions, and I allow Him to tell me the truth so that I can be effective.

The flight attendant started to tear up and cry, and she gave her life to the Lord! She went and told the captain. "Did you hear that Kevin died on the operating table?" The captain then came to me, "You never told me you died." I had known him for 15-20 years. I said, "Well, I do not want to force it on anybody." The pilot then asked me to come up to the cockpit during the next flight to hear all about it. I went to the cockpit during the flight, and the captain turned around and started talking to me. The first officers were there, one person flies the plane, and the other person monitors the radios. The captain was looking at me, so I started to tell him my story. He said, "My God!" It changed him immediately at seven miles up and going 600 miles an hour. He was changed because something from the other realm touched him while I was talking. Now, the first officer was visibly moved, and the captain looked at him and said, "You need to hear this. I have the airplane." The first officer turned around to me, and he was crying. He said, "While you were talking, I had an open vision, and I do not even believe in this stuff." He said, "I was in the woods when I was 16 years old, and Jesus was there. Someone had accidentally shot an arrow towards the back of my head while we were hunting. I heard my name called, and I turned around, and I caught the arrow before it went into my eye. My friends, including the one who shot it by accident, saw it happen. They all said no one called my name out, but I heard my name. The arrow should have hit me in the back of the head and gone through my skull. I could not tell you, until this day, why I was able to turn around and catch that arrow because even if you knew it was coming, you could not catch it. Just now, while you were talking, Jesus appeared to me and said, 'The only reason you are alive is that today is your day of salvation. I sent this man to tell you the way, receive Me.'"

What is the "ministry of reconciliation" and how did you come to have it? Why is it so important?

_____
_____
_____
_____

- ❖ We have the ministry of reconciliation, and Jesus said, "Compel them to come in" (see Luke 14:23). We are to compel people. We talk to people and inform them that the price has been paid and to come in.

  - Jesus is not going to come back and die again. He made sure that He scraped the bottom of hell because He was not doing it again.
  - There are no amendments; there is no cleanup. Jesus did it all, *once and for all*, He paid the price for *everyone* (1 Peter 3:18).
  - The people in hell right now should not be there, but they are.
  - There is a hell, and people are there being tormented, and their books in Heaven show that a great plan of salvation was theirs.
  - Do you understand that the conversation I had with Jesus was how do I get people to see their need when they don't see it? And how do I turn a whole generation if I go back? How do I turn a generation who does not see their need for Christ?

- ❖ **Revelation 3:17-18** "Because you say, 'I am rich, have become wealthy, and have need of nothing'—and do not know that you are wretched, miserable, poor, blind, and naked—I counsel you to buy from Me gold refined in the fire, that you may be rich; and white garments, that you may be clothed, *that* the shame of your nakedness may not be revealed; and anoint your eyes with eye salve, that you may see."

  - Jesus showed me in the book of Revelation when He was talking to the seven churches how He addressed the churches.
  - To one of the churches, Jesus said, "You say you are rich and well clothed, and you can see. But the truth is you are wretched, miserable, poor, blind, and naked."
  - Jesus was telling them the truth. He said, if they knew what was right, they would ask for eye salve, a robe of righteousness and gold that was tried in the fire.

- Jesus always has provision, and He has the answer for what you need.
- Unfortunately, you are not asking for the right things.
- You stay in neutral, which means you are going downstream fast.

What did Jesus mean in Revelation 3:17 when He counsels you to buy gold from Him refined in the fire and white garments?

_____
_____
_____
_____

KNOW YOUR ENEMY

❖ The spirit of this world is going to continue to pull on you, and the spirit of the world is strong. You have got to know your enemy.

- **Warrior Note:** What you *do not know* can hurt you, and what you *do know* may hurt you if it is *wrong* information.
- If you are acting on false information or you are operating without knowledge, you will be injured, or worse.
- I can name ministers who have died in jet crashes.
- If I had been their pilot, I would have walked away and told them to get another pilot.
- I would not have been taking that airplane anywhere because I would have looked at the reports. The planes needed repairs and should have stayed in the hangar. The Ministers took off in them, and the body of Christ was robbed of their gifts.
- God is not mocked.

THE NOTES OF A WARRIOR

- ❖ The plane crashes and loss of life were satan's devices to cause questions in every Christian's mind.

    - Why is it that I have flown six flights a day for 30 years and never had a crash? It is because God is not mocked; a man reaps what he sows. I know that there are inspections that go on every night with each aircraft. I know that there is an inspection that happens every month. I know there is an expert inspection that happens every year, and there is a D-check which happens every 15 years where they completely refurbish the airplane. Sometimes it is 20 years. I can pray for the pilot, and I can pray for the mechanic. I am not going down in an airplane. The company monitors each person that inspects, and all are committed to doing their job. If they do their job, that airplane will continue to fly. There are very few airplanes that fall out of the sky. Why is it that after 30 years, thirty-seven million miles, not one crash, and not one smoking hole? It is the mercy of God; it is the grace of God. However, know that we prayed for every person involved. The Angels make sure that each person does their job; they monitor the situation.

- ❖ I do not throw my life up to chance, and I am reaping what I am sowing. I think if you could find a way to check it out, you would find that people are reaping what they are sowing.

    - You ask why this minister? Why did that happen? I know what happened, and it is not God's fault. A man reaps what he sows.
    - "For he who sows to the flesh will of the flesh reap corruption, but he who sows to the Spirit will of the Spirit reap everlasting life" (Galatians 6:8).
    - You have heard God's word, and it is the truth about the matter.

Where in your life have you been sowing to the flesh? Repent and begin to sow to the Spirit in order to reap the fruit of the Spirit.

_____
_____
_____
_____

- ❖ Jesus wants one person to side with Him and change a generation. He needs one person, one crazy person that will recklessly abandon themselves.

    - Those kinds of people are heroes in the next generation, but they are hated by the generation in which they live.
    - You want to know why? It is because everybody migrates toward comfort.
    - Every generation needs a prophetic voice because the prophets are weeping while people are laughing, and they are laughing while people are weeping because they are way ahead.
    - When I was in the future, I saw how the prophetic works.
    - God takes prophets to the future and then puts them back in the present.
    - The standards, for a generation, are determined by their future.
    - The Word of God is transforming because it is not from this realm.
    - Holy men of old were moved by the Holy Spirit and wrote.
    - That is how you got the Word of God. It did not originate from man.
    - It was a supernatural encounter that somebody had then they wrote — moved by the Holy Spirit, not by their flesh.

CHAPTER 4

The Origin and Operation of Your Enemy

"Have I therefore become your enemy because I tell you the truth?"
Galatians 4:16

DISCUSSION:

The enemy knows that he has got to keep you in the flesh. Living in the flesh and reaping the flesh keeps you out of your everyday supernatural briefing from Heaven. I am not kidding you. Every day is an experience, but it has already happened long ago. I am playing out what I already saw, I show up, just like you show up, and it is all scripted. The devil does not want Christians to hear any of this. What does God do? He chooses someone who is retired who decides to go into the ministry and does not have an agenda. He does not need anything and shows up even if people do not like him. It doesn't matter to me; I will show up. You have to get to the place as Paul said, "Have I therefore become your enemy because I tell you the truth" (Galatians 4:16). You see, a generation needs to hear the truth, but it is forward-looking. It is causing the perception to change so that this generation sets it up for the next generation.

- ❖ We do not need to have another move of God. We need to maintain the move of God that began when Jesus breathed on the disciples, and then the Holy Spirit came on the day of Pentecost.

  - We need to *maintain* that move. It started on the day of Pentecost as mighty wind and fire, utterance, and drunkenness in the Holy Spirit.

- Do not forget the fact that on Pentecost, they were all in unity, which is the biggest miracle of all. You had one hundred and twenty people in unity. You cannot get six people to agree on anything today.
- You had five things that happened when the Holy Spirit came.
- Look at us now! We are so sophisticated, and we know how to maintain our composure.
- If I leave a service, and people are not lying on the floor laughing, I feel disappointed because that is one of the manifestations, being drunk in the Holy Spirit.
- If the fire is not burning in you, as I am talking, I am disappointed.
- That is how the Holy Spirit introduced Himself to us as a person, wind, fire, utterance, and drunkenness.
- The Holy Spirit in power is the church of the Living God, and we are temples of the Holy Spirit

❖ **1 Corinthians 6:19-20** "Or do you not know that your body is the temple of the Holy Spirit *who is* in you, whom you have from God, and you are not your own? For you were bought at a price; therefore glorify God in your body and in your spirit, which are God's."

- Paul said our bodies are not our own. We have been bought with a price. Our life is not our own.
- It is as though Jesus is borrowing our body, and He is living His ministry through us. That is absolute truth.
- Yes, I will fast and pray for another move of God with you. But the move of God has begun.
- If you talk to angels, it has never ended. They are the ones that believe in you more than you believe in yourself; they would not even bother with you unless the Lord God had sent them.
- They believe in you because they are told that you are the chosen ones; you are the sons and daughters of God. You are the elect.

THE NOTES OF A WARRIOR

How can you glorify God in your body and your spirit?

_____
_____
_____
_____

- ❖ Your enemy, satan, knows that a Christian that is misinformed or not informed is a non-event. He knows they are Christians that do not feed themselves on the Word of God and do not drink of the Spirit of God from the river of life, and he has them.

    - These Christians do not allow the river of life to come up from within them and yield to it because it gives life.
    - Life is in the blood, life is in the river, and life is in the breath. These things are what you should dwell on as a Christian.
    - The enemy does not want you to hear anything I just said, which is why I am going to go deeper.
    - If you knew how vile your enemy is or how intent he is, you would turn your whole life over to God.
    - You would not be compromised any longer because the greatest power you have against satan is being fully yielded to God.
    - Your power is based on your unwavering faith, which is your trust, which is ignited by the fire from the altar of God, and it is a holy fire.
    - You set yourself apart, and you have become a different person because Christ is living through you.

- ❖ **<u>Warrior Note</u>: Holy fire is something satan hates because he cannot function in it; it paralyzes him. Your whole goal should be to be immersed in fire and fully yielded to God.**

    - Be placed in a situation where you are completely engulfed in holy fire. You will then have a message of reconciliation wherever you go.

- You have only to inform people that their sins have been paid if they acknowledge Jesus Christ as being the person who paid off their debt.
- As long as they recognize Jesus, then He becomes the way. He is the door, so you have to tell people this (see John 14:6).
- You take people out of the hands of satan when you do that. The Lord does not want us to wait any longer.
- God is convinced of what He has already planned, and now it is time *for us* to be fully convinced of His plan.
- We do not rest on our abilities. We rest on God's ability through us, which means that you have to be yielded.

What is stopping you from witnessing to others about God's plan of redemption?

_____
_____
_____
_____

BEFORE THE FLOOD

❖ I was not allowed to talk about this until this year, but this was shown to me back in 1992. It is incredible how everywhere I go now, I release new information that I have never been able to share before, but it is time.

- What you are dealing with is disembodied spirits of people that lived before the flood who had interbred.
- Before the flood, everyone in the whole race of human beings had interbred, (see Genesis 6:1-2) except Noah and his family, eight in all.
- No one except Noah was completely perfect in his generation (see Genesis 6:8-9), and he walked with God.

- There were millions of people on earth, and none of them were invited to go on the ark. The dinosaurs were hybrids and did not get invited.
- All of those spirits from before the flood had no redemption and no resurrection because they did not qualify. Welcome to your enemy.

DISCUSSION:

The fallen ones were under Hillel, who became Lucifer. Hillel was over the garden. One day a man came into the garden. Hillel saw that God would come down and visit the man Adam and speak with him. God did not even look at Hillel. This cherub, Hillel, could see that Adam looked like God. The last time Hillel looked at himself, he did not look like God. He watched God give Adam authority over everything. Hillel was the anointed cherub that covered over Eden, and now he was out of a job.

❖ **John 8:44** "You are of *your* father the devil, and the desires of your father you want to do. He was a murderer from the beginning, and does not stand in the truth, because there is no truth in him. When he speaks a lie, he speaks from his own *resources,* for he is a liar and the father of it."

- Things turned in my life when I accepted the truth.
- The truth of it is demons hate you because they are out, and you are in.
- They lie like their father, the devil, and the religious system is hooked up to that because Jesus said they were liars, just like their father.
- The devil was a liar from the beginning.
- These spirits hate you because they disqualified themselves.
- There were not that many fallen angels.
- There were only a few angels that came and fell because they have the honor system.

- They were under Hillel, they fell, and they have no redemption, and they are chained right now until the end times.

2 Peter 2:4 "For if God did not spare the angels who sinned, but cast *them* down to hell and delivered *them* into chains of darkness, to be reserved for judgment;"

- The angels that left their abode (see Jude 1:6) are chained, and they are not the demons.
- Peter says here that those angels are chained. So, what are the demons? They are rogue spirits that are against God from before the flood.
- These demons hate God, and they hate you, and they are going to work to make sure that you are disqualified if it is possible.
- At the very end, even the elect will be deceived if that is possible (see Matthew (24:24). Now, this is your enemy.
- The world was destroyed in the flood because of sexual sin.
- The sons of God went into the daughters of men (see Genesis 6:4) and had mighty ones as children.
- The Nephilim were on the earth in those days, but it does not say the Nephilim interbred.

Jesus said in Matthew 24:24 that if possible, even the elect might be deceived. How can you protect yourself from being deceived?

_____
_____
_____
_____

THE NOTES OF A WARRIOR

HAND YOURSELF OVER TO GOD

I did not want to come back to this earth because it is so stacked against you. You cannot live a mediocre neutral Christian life; it is impossible. It is impossible to have Christ in you, the hope of glory, and not be able to be a demon buster!

- <u>**Colossians 1:27**</u> "To them God willed to make known what are the riches of the glory of this mystery among the Gentiles: which is Christ in you, the hope of glory."

    - You cannot live in this life and be ineffective if you have Christ in you. It is impossible, yet it is happening because God is being mocked.
    - You reap what you sow, so you have to sow toward your spiritual life.
    - If you do not want to do it for yourself, will you please do it for the body of Christ? Will you please do it for me; help me.
    - I tell people if you do not want to prosper, then don't, but would you thrive for the body? Would you prosper so that we can get this done and let Jesus come back? Get the harvest to come in.
    - Would you believe in healing just so that you can stay on this earth and wrap it up with us, instead of going home early?
    - What I am saying is that we think we are so holy and religious. However, we are selfish in our inability to accept the benefits and responsibilities of what God has given us.
    - **Do you understand that this is why Christianity is not attractive to the world, it is because we do not display Jesus as He really is?**

- Why is it that when I show up in the cockpit, all of a sudden, the pieces of the puzzle start falling into place over something that happened to someone at the age of 16 on a hunting accident?

    - It was set up for me to be there at that company.

- I left the ministry to go work for an airline, and the whole time I was there, 30 years, I thought I did something wrong because I was in the world working instead of being in a pulpit somewhere.
- Little did I know that the cockpit became my pulpit. The plane became my pulpit, and everywhere I went, became my pulpit.
- Now I find myself in a pulpit, and I do not even want to be in the pulpit. I want to be on my back porch in retirement.
- **That is why I got the pulpit. It is the only reason I got the pulpit because I do not want it.**

❖ **Warrior Note: You are handed life because you allowed yourself to experience death. You experience resurrection because you die.**

- Hand yourself over to God so that you can have the ministry of reconciliation.
- Then everywhere you go, it shifts the atmosphere, and satan cannot handle you.
- No matter what the devil sends at you, the demons will come back weeping, "We can't penetrate him; we can't get to her."
- Why is that? It is the fact that you are informed. You have the correct information, and you have the vision of Heaven.
- People need to know what they are dealing with on this earth.

What do you have to do to carry out the ministry of reconciliation?

_____
_____
_____
_____

THE NOTES OF A WARRIOR

THE REVELATION OF THE SONS OF GOD

We only see one-sixth of the available light, which are the colors of the rainbow. The five-sixths that we are missing from our eyes is due to the fall of man. That does not mean it ceases to exist because you cannot see it. It is the same thing with your hearing; your dog hears more than you do. We used to hear everything. My friend was an astronaut, and he flew out of the atmosphere, and it is all classified, He has friends that walked on the moon. He said that outside of the earth's atmosphere there are no demons. He said on the moon, his friend Neil Armstrong would have devotions with God, and before he would finish asking God a question, Neil said that God would answer him as clear as you and I talk. My friend who flew out of the atmosphere said there are no demons out there. There is nothing to stop you from hearing God's voice. It is down here that there is a war. God is still speaking to you; you do not hear it because there is so much concentrated effort against you. There are demons packed in here on the earth. They are left over from the flood, and they are against you. They are trapped here. When Jesus would show up, they would plead with Him not to send them out of the area because this is where they were before the flood. They have created a matrix, a system, a government, and they fight each other. They do not even get along with each other. They will fight each other over territories, and I have seen it happen. I am serious. If you want to feel freedom from what is buffeting you, go to a border. Those demons will not be allowed to go with you. Then you will have to deal with all the demons over there, but it will be different than what you are dealing with here.

- ❖ In your authority as a believer, you can create a border in your own home, and you do not have to go physically out of the area to get rid of oppression.

  - You can establish your own borders and your own authority, and the demons will know that you know your authority.
  - I see white flags being raised all the time because the demons will opt-out rather than fight. The sons of God are being revealed.

- Now, who are you?
- You have been designated as a son and a daughter of God.
- You are the children of God.
- You cannot change what the grace of God has already done for you.
- However, you can slow down the maturity process by not cooperating.
- That is why my wife and I are doing what we are doing. We are not ministering because we need to or have to.
- We are doing this because Heaven has determined that if we do this, it will change a whole generation.
- God designated all of this before I was born.

How do you avoid oppression from demonic spirits?

_____
_____
_____
_____

- ❖ **Romans 8:19-21** "For the earnest expectation of the creation eagerly waits for the revealing of the sons of God. For the creation was subjected to futility, not willingly, but because of Him who subjected *it* in hope; because the creation itself also will be delivered from the bondage of corruption into the glorious liberty of the children of God."

  - God also designated that the last generation on the earth would be history makers—every single one of them.
  - Every person on the earth that walks with God will be known, not just known by God; the world will know them.
  - The sons of God will be revealed in these last days.

- **Daniel 12:3** "Those who are wise shall shine like the brightness of the firmament, and those who turn many to righteousness like the stars forever and ever."

    - The bright and shining ones (see Daniel 12:3), the righteous will shine like the noonday sun (see Psalm 37:6 AMP). It is already happening.
    - It happened to Moses in the Old Testament under an old covenant because Moses went up to the mountain and met with God continually, 40 days at a time.
    - His face started to be transformed back to what Adam looked like in the garden. His face began to shine light out of it. The Israelites had Moses cover his face because they were afraid to look at him.
    - Moses saw his face revert to Adams by his association with God and being up there with the Holy One, and that was under the *Old Covenant*. How much more the New Covenant.

- I was told by my Savior that if I go back, I cannot lose, it is all rigged in my favor, and I cannot fail. As soon as I came back, God started hooking me up with the right people. I have more fathers in the faith that are generals. I needed one general, and I now have several.

    - You cannot fail. God is going to hook you up. He is going to hook you up with people that will blaze the trail for you.
    - There is an eight-lane highway, but someone had a machete in their hands and paved the way for us. Jesus paved the way for us. He sent people ahead of you to pave the way for you.
    - There are plenty of highways in the Spirit that are already paved for us. We do not need to reinvent the Gospel; we need to live it, and have it manifest in our lives.
    - We have more to help us build our faith than any other generation did. It is not the building of our faith; it is the manifestation that we need.

If you cannot fail, then what are you afraid of?

_____
_____
_____
_____

ACCEPTED IN THE BELOVED

You have got to know your enemy. He is the one that is holding it back. Once you get rid of him, it is amazing how free you become. Eliminate his influence in your life. I have seen transformation every week for the 30 years that I flew with Southwest Airlines. Every week I had three days with a set of employees that I would work with. On that third day, there was such a transformation in those people's lives. I found that they either hated me and wanted to kill me, or they loved me, and there was no in-between. If the person decided not to flow with what God had designed for that week for them, then they got worse. I saw almost 90 percent of the people turn to God because, on that third day, that demon would leave them. I did not cast it out; I talked to them, and I loved on them. I used to tell myself that they do not hate me; they do not know me, and I would not allow anyone to defeat me through rejection because I am not rejected.

- ❖ **Ephesians 1:5-6** "having predestined us to adoption as sons by Jesus Christ to Himself, according to the good pleasure of His will, to the praise of the glory of His grace, by which He made us accepted in the Beloved."

    - Satan has three easy plans he uses to defeat you
    - **First, satan's design is to keep information from you.**
    - **Second, if he gets you the information, he wants it to be the wrong information.**
    - **Third, what satan wants is for you to live in rejection.**
    - However, God says, "He made you accepted in the beloved."

THE NOTES OF A WARRIOR

How can you overcome the three plans satan uses to defeat you?

_____
_____
_____
_____
_____

- ❖ **Romans 8:15** TPT "And you did not receive the "spirit of religious duty," leading you back into the fear *of never being good enough*. But you have received the "Spirit of full acceptance," enfolding you into the family of God. And you will never feel orphaned, for as he rises up within us, our spirits join him in saying the words of tender affection, "Beloved Father!"

    - You have received the "Spirit of full acceptance."
    - You are loved and accepted.
    - **Now, there is power in your relationship with God.**

- ❖ We are the manifest sons of God. That means you cannot hide under a bowl. You are light. There is nothing physically on this earth that can hide the light of God. God supersedes all of that.

    - Demons cannot stand it when people see the light, and they understand God's love for them.
    - You have to provide answers even if people are not asking because they do need God.
    - What people want, if you talk to them, is they want manifestation. People want to know what I have that they do not have.
    - What I found is that everyone wants to believe that there is a God.
    - Everyone wants to believe that there is a supernatural realm that is beyond this realm.

According to Romans 8:15 TPT, as a born-again Christian, why should you never feel orphaned? How does this Word empower you?

_____
_____
_____
_____

CHAPTER 5

Know No Limits

"Everything we could ever need for life and complete devotion to God has already been deposited in us by his divine power. For all this was lavished upon us through the rich experience of knowing him who has called us by name and invited us to come to him through a glorious manifestation of His goodness." 2 Peter 1:3 TPT

DISCUSSION:

My message for this realm is that God Himself took the limitations off through Jesus Christ. I saw my limitations down here, and I was so upset that I had allowed this world's spirit to dictate what I can and cannot do. You see, every person wants to believe that there is a place where they are not limited. There were two men Orville and Wilbur that looked up and saw birds flying, and they wanted to do it. It just about killed them trying, but they did it. Men tried to break a four-minute mile and could not do it. And then, one week, somebody accidentally did, and the next week, three or four people broke it, and this is the way it works. Someone has to supersede the limitations to give permission to other people to do it. Jesus sent somebody back from the dead to tell people. This whole thing was a setup for you before you were born. Every single human being on this earth has this setup. Jesus told me I could not have made a mistake because he was three feet from me. Jesus said that everyone is written in a book in Heaven before they were born, and everyone's book shows them coming to Heaven (see Psalm 139:16). No one is ever designed to go to hell.

- **Matthew 25:41** "Then He will also say to those on the left hand, 'Depart from Me, you cursed, into the everlasting fire prepared for the devil and his angels:"

  - Hell, according to Jesus, was made for the devil and his angels, not for man. If Jesus said that, I believe Him.
  - When I was on the other side, I saw that demonic influence in this realm is what causes us to stay in a small place.
  - You can know the truth, and the truth *should* set you free.
  - The wavering comes in the mental realm because we are not entirely convinced.
  - Faith is of the heart. It is of your spirit, and it is not from your head.

If hell was created for the devil and his angels, why do people go to hell?

_____
_____
_____
_____

- **Mark 11:23-24** "For assuredly, I say to you, whoever says to this mountain, 'Be removed and be cast into the sea,' and does not doubt in his heart, but believes that those things he says will be done, he will have whatever he says. Therefore I say to you, whatever things you ask when you pray, believe that you receive *them,* and you will have *them.*"

  - Jesus said when you pray, you should believe *before* you receive it.
  - He said when you see a mountain, you should believe in your heart that what you say with your mouth, not believe in your *head.*
  - Believe in your *heart* that what you say with your mouth shall come to pass, and you shall have it.

- Faith is of the *heart*. Your heart is the real you.
- The spirit of man is the candle of the Lord (see proverbs 20:27 KJV).

❖ I saw this; our limitations are based on the fact that we fell, and this earth realm limits us. Six is the number of man. We see 1/6th of light. It was not meant to be that way. We are in a fallen world.

❖ **How did Christ Jesus cause us to triumph?**
  - **He took hold of us before we needed Him.**
  - **He adopted us before we were born.**
  - **He provided for us before we existed.**
  - **The time realm limits us from understanding this.**

❖ <u>**Ephesians 2:10**</u> TPT "We have become his poetry, a re-created people that will fulfill the destiny he has given each of us, for we are joined to Jesus, the Anointed One. Even before we were born, God planned in advance *our destiny* and the good works we would do *to fulfill it*!"

- According to Paul, God even established all the good works that we would do in Christ before the foundations of the world.
- According to Paul, he was designated as an apostle at birth. He was already designated, but he killed Christians.
- Paul had them killed, probably until he was in his thirties. He still said, "I wronged no man." Maybe Stephen would have a say so in that because Paul had him killed.
- Paul said he had wronged no man. Well, how could he say that?
- He had a revelation that *all the limitations had been taken off*.

- In Christ, Paul had never sinned. He accepted Jesus Christ, and his file was utterly disintegrated and gone. It does not exist in Heaven.
- No one up there is going to remind you of what you did wrong. There is no account of it. I encountered all this in Heaven.

What did Jesus say you must do to receive what you pray for?

_____
_____
_____
_____

DISCUSSION:

When I was 19 years old, I got saved, and Jesus came to me and explained to me my five-fold calling. He told me, "This is what you are called to do." Jesus said to me, "You are going to go to college, and then you are going to work for an airline. When you retire from the airline, you are going to go into the ministry." That all happened. Jesus said, "I do not want you being manipulated by money because your message could be manipulated if people stopped giving to you." That is what he told me at 19 years old. I can show you the spot on the hill in Pennsylvania, where He came to me. Jesus said, "Due to your calling, people are not going to like you. I am going to give you a career so that you are never going to have to worry about money again." Everybody is trying to reverse engineer me. They do not understand that I did not start this thing, and I am not finishing it. It was already wrapped up before I was even in the know about Christianity. I did not even know about the born-again experience. Someone had to tell me that it was also in the Bible. My pastor never told me, and because of that lack of information, I was not operating at my full potential. As soon as I learned that you need to be born again, I immediately went home, got on my knees, and became born again. It did not need to take that long.

- When Jesus said this is what you are going to do, this is who you are, and this is what will happen, I did not wait. I adopted that immediately, and my path was set.

- **You cannot be ignited enough with the passion of the fire that is from the altar of God. There is not enough to fix me; I need more. No matter what I get, I need more. I need more fire. I need more because it helps me to overcome my enemy.**

- <u>2 Corinthians 12:9-10</u> "And He said to me, 'My grace is sufficient for you, for My strength is made perfect in weakness.' Therefore most gladly I will rather boast in my infirmities, that the power of Christ may rest upon me. Therefore I take pleasure in infirmities, in reproaches, in needs, in persecutions, in distresses, for Christ's sake. For when I am weak, then I am strong."

    - Paul said the power of God is revealed in his weakness.
    - Paul gloried in his weakness.
    - The ploy of the enemy is to get you self-sufficient.
    - satan always tries to get you to have a plan B and a plan C, instead of God's perfect plan for you.
    - "If God is not big enough, you can always help Him out" the devil whispers.
    - The enemy does not want you to put your trust in God.
    - Well, how do you explain me? I believed God.
    - I am not doing this for myself, but I am an example.
    - I am a testimony to you that *God wants you to encounter Him all the time.*

Why do you think God's strength is made perfect in your weakness?

_____
_____
_____
_____

- ❖ The way God gets you to encounter Him all the time is by you working with Him, and only Him, and no middleman.

    - I do not need someone to pray for me; *I need to pray*.
    - When I need money, *I go to work*. I pray the whole way there, and I pray the whole way home.
    - If you do that, then one day, you too will work yourself out of a job.
    - When I am sick, I take medicine, but I am praying the whole time believing for my healing.
    - I am not compromising because I want to stay alive, and I want to be happy while I am doing it.
    - Understand that you are on your way to healing. You are on your way to financial stability.
    - I am going to pray in tongues in the ambulance if I end up in an ambulance, but I am not planning on it.
    - I do not get knocked out because God is not mocked.
    - There is a bright shining door in every dark situation. There is an answer to every question you have.

How does God get you to encounter Him all the time? When you need something, what should you do?

_____
_____
_____
_____

THE NOTES OF A WARRIOR

SEATED IN HEAVENLY PLACES

- ❖ I was at the throne of God, and you can try as hard as you can, you cannot think of one question to ask. I had done my best, and I could not think of a thing that I wanted to know.

    - Do you want to know why? Jesus told me, "There are no questions at the throne, only answers."
    - He said, "That is why you should come here all the time. Just go ahead and be seated here with Me in the Heavenly realms."

- ❖ **Ephesians 2:6** "And raised *us* up together, and made *us* sit together in the Heavenly *places* in Christ Jesus,"

- ❖ **Colossians 3:1** "If then you were raised with Christ, seek those things which are above, where Christ is, sitting at the right hand of God."

- ❖ **Revelation 3:21** "To him who overcomes I will grant to sit with Me on My throne, as I also overcame and sat down with My Father on His throne."

    - There are no questions at the throne. Come up and be seated.
    - There are some silly things down here on earth.
    - We have focused on the cross, but how many have a pendant on their necklace that is an empty tomb?
    - You need to go on and be seated with Him; this is your future, and this is your now. It is how you should live every day.
    - Please do not spend the next 20 years finding out what I am telling you is true. It is all in the Scriptures.

THE HOLY OF HOLIES

DISCUSSION:

I was with Jesus for forty-five minutes in Heaven, the Holy Spirit, who is a person, was behind me. He was telling me the seven different levels of every Word that Jesus was speaking to me. Jesus was in front of me, the Father was seated on a throne being worshipped, and the Holy Spirit was behind me. He was telling me Old Testament Scripture after Scripture about the types and shadows of everything that Jesus was saying. And Jesus was quoting Himself as though it was His first time saying it. He was quoting the Scripture. Can you imagine for forty-five minutes Jesus quoting Himself? It should have been enough for me to open my Bible every day and eat His Word daily. However, I had to die, meet Him, have Him quote Himself for forty-five minutes, and then send me back. The time is running out, and we are no longer in the kiddie pool in training.

- **Warrior Note: Psalm 91:1 "He who dwells in the secret place of the Most High shall abide under the shadow of the Almighty."**

- When I came back, it was the hardest thing for me because I felt like there is such a distance between what I know and what I have to relay to people. So that what I experienced people can experience.

  - There is such a gap, but Jesus closed the gap by opening up the Holy of Holies. We are to go into the Holy of Holies; *it is the secret place.*
  - It is in the shadow of the cherubim's wings — the Most High God.
  - God does not have wings, but His cherubim do. We are to be under the wings of the Most High, and that is under the wings of the cherubim that cover Him (see Psalm 91:4).

- The throne room looks just like the model that Moses built for the tabernacle. God is seated on the Mercy Seat with cherubim on both sides of Him.
- If you can get really close at an angle to one of those cherubim, you will fall in the shadow of the Most High God.
- If you stay there and make that your dwelling place, according to Psalm 91:1-16, none of these things are going to touch you, and they are all listed here. It is not a drive-thru window; you must *dwell* there.
- God is not mocked if you make the Most High your dwelling place.
- The secret place *is* the dwelling place.

Read Psalm 91 and make a list of the things that will not touch you when you dwell in the secret place of the Most High.

_____
_____
_____
_____

❖ You go into the Holy of Holies, and you pronounce the name of God, just like the High Priest did in the temple. When you go in there and announce the name of God, you can stay there.

- That name above all names is Yehoshua, Jesus.
- Is there any name that is above His name? Then why would a High Priest say something else?
- Jesus is the name above all names.
- The High Priests announced His name once a year with blood.
- In Hebrew, it is Joshua, Yehoshua.

- ❖ **Philippians 2:9-11** "Therefore God also has highly exalted Him and given Him the name which is above every name, that at the name of Jesus every knee should bow, of those in heaven, and of those on earth, and of those under the earth, and *that* every tongue should confess that Jesus Christ *is* Lord, to the glory of God the Father."

- ❖ I could not ask any questions about the Trinity when I was in Heaven. Do you want to know why? It was because I understood the whole thing.

  - Now that I am back, it takes me hours to explain it.
  - I understood Einstein and all his theories when I came back from Heaven. I understood UFOs and dinosaurs. I understood it all.
  - I understood how to play instruments without having lessons. I could look at something and reverse engineer it.
  - I could touch a door handle that someone else had just touched and know that in a year, they are going to be dead.
  - Then I have to ask God, "Should I tell them, or should I leave it?"
  - Sometimes He says, "Do not to say a word because they are going to be held accountable for it."
  - I have been told not to tell people things because they are going to be judged for that word because they are not going to listen to it.

ADDRESS YOUR ENEMY

- ❖ Did you know that God could tell you to do something, and it could go wrong? The reason why is because you have got to address your enemy.

  - The enemy has come to steal, kill, and destroy, and he does not stop just because God told you to do something.
  - God is speaking to you right now, but your relationship is not based on your car not starting in the morning.

- What did I do wrong, God? You know I spent the whole morning listening to Kevin and now my car's broken, and I have a flat tire. Or all of the sudden your refrigerator is broken.
- You do not base your relationship on God by these things that happen.
- It has nothing to do with that. *You have an enemy, and you have to address that enemy.*
- The enemy is going to work against what God has told you. If you do not stop him, he will continue to drive you to defeat and into a corner.
- *You have to address him.* You need to be rough with him. Do you know how many meals I've missed so that I can give him a headache?
- I have walked away from what I wanted so that I can drive devils out.
- I have refused to take jobs that paid four times what I was making because God did not have that path for me.
- I got to drive devils out by doing what I was called to do.

❖ **Warrior Note: satan does not know how to deal with somebody who is completely submitted to God, who is obedient and has no rebellion in them.**

- satan does not understand that. He is a fallen being.
- I was shown that lucifer (Hillel) ate from the tree, and he fell, and he was the one that deceived man. He was deceived, and there was no one to tempt him, he had no reason to fall.
- satan's eyes were open; that is why he hates you. He fell first, and he could not get to Adam, so he isolated Eve.
- This whole thing happened because of one being who left his abode, who was not satisfied with what he was given (see Jude 6).
- Because of this, we and all creation are suffering; it is time to make the devil suffer.
- He stole God's creation; stole from God. It is time to make him pay.

DISCUSSION:

Lucifer's eyes were open, and he saw the difference between good and evil, and he could not handle it. He knew that we could not either. We would always make the wrong choice because we are not God. Do you understand that God is the only one that can know the difference between good and evil and still choose good? We are made in His image, but we are not God. We are not the original. If we know the difference between good and evil, we cannot choose good. Only God could do that. That is why God put that tree in the garden, to remind man that He is God and we are not. That "being" trespassed, and he fell and iniquity was found in him. He was perfect; it says, "You were the seal of perfection" (see Ezekiel 28:12b). It is time to make him pay. You make the devil pay by turning everything he is giving you—you give it back to him, and he becomes the victim. satan does not want people to know this. You have got to make it hard for him. The first thing I did this morning was to remind him of the lake of fire. I was told that every morning wherever I go to remind the enemy that I am driving him and his cohorts out today. I give demons a heads up in case they want to vacate on their own without a fight. When are other people going to start talking like this?

How do you make the devil pay for what he is doing in your life?

_____
_____
_____
_____

- ❖ The Jesus I met started crying when He told me what He had suffered for me with what He went through.

- When I came back, do you know what He made me do? He made me watch *The Passion of the Christ* movie, just the part where He started to get beaten until He died on the cross.
- I had to watch that 33 times, and you know, after watching it for a while, I think twice about sinning willfully.
- Jesus started crying because we did not discern what He had gone through for us. We did not discern that He had bought us and that He had paved the way for us to be victorious warriors.
- He has allowed us to constantly go from victory to victory, never losing an inch of ground because He bought it all for us.
- Once you see this, do not wait until you get to Heaven to grasp these realities. This life is broken, and this world is broken.
- Jesus has given you life, so glorify God in the flesh. You do everything for Him, and set your heart fully on what He has for you.

❖ I saw the futures of so many people; they are so bright. Your futures put together are so bright you cannot even look at it. You have been ushered into a greater revelation of who Jesus is to you. Jesus wept when He told me that people did not discern, He choked up; He could hardly talk to me.

- Jesus just wanted people to know that He had gone to the depths of hell and bought every person back.
- He took me to the blue sapphire stones that are all over the throne room floor. It was thick sapphire blue with white flames going through it.
- The stones were living, and Jesus said, "Enoch was allowed to walk on these stones. Hillel used to walk on these."
- I went to walk on them, and Jesus said, "This is by invitation only."
- I said, "Lord, you have made me righteous you have made me holy."
- Jesus said, "This is not positional, Kevin, this is relational, and it is for those who walk in fear of the Lord on the earth."

- I said, "Lord, I have not been taught this." He said, "There is relational, and there is positional, and this sapphire is relational."
- Then Jesus took me to the outside. I do not know how to explain it, but He took me way out, and there was a fence.
- All the Christians were around the fence the whole way around.
- Jesus said, "This separates the Kingdom of God and the spirit of the world."
- He said, "My people, instead of asking where the hottest spot in Heaven is, which is that sapphire. They want to know where the fence is so they can live in the world and still get to Heaven."
- Jesus was weeping. He said, "I did not die for that fence. I died for this sapphire so that My people could walk on the sapphire stones."

Is there any area of your life where you are sitting on "the fence" with one foot in the world? Take time now to repent and strengthen your relationship with the Lord.

_____
_____
_____
_____

- ❖ **Exodus 24:10-11** "And they saw the God of Israel. And *there was* under His feet as it were a paved work of sapphire stone, and it was like the very Heavens in *its* clarity. But on the nobles of the children of Israel He did not lay His hand. So they saw God, and they ate and drank."

- In Exodus 24:10 God came down on the mountain and stood before the 70 elders as they ate. He stood there, and He did not judge them on the sapphire platform.
- Remember how important you are and that you have been bought.
- However, it is much more than what you are being told. I do not understand why I had to die and come back to tell you this.
- I am telling you so that you can see that right now; your future is bright. It is beyond even hope, and I saw that things are sealed.
- However, you must remember that if you do not take care of the enemy by driving him out, he will influence the outcome, and it is not God's will.

❖ Think about Paul. He said, "Corinthians, I long to come to you, but satan hindered me."

- Paul was an apostle of all apostles, and he was hindered by satan.
- Jesus, in His own hometown, was hindered from doing the will of the Father because of their unbelief (see Matthew 13:58).

Why was Jesus not able to do any major miracles in His hometown?
_____
_____
_____
_____

Father, in the name of Jesus, thank you for the impartation of your Spirit. Thank you for rising up in us, causing us to take hold of that which Christ has taken hold of for us. That we go toward the mark, the high calling of God in Christ Jesus, and we grasp the realities of being in You. We live, and we move, and we have our being in You.

The Holy Spirit wants to say through me, "The God you know is going to show up, and you watch what happens in your life." The Spirit of God is saying, "I am rising up big inside of you." He is calling you, "Mighty ones." He is saying, "I am rising up big in you O mighty ones of God."

The Lord has succeeded in winning you over. May the face of God Himself shine upon you, and may He smile upon you in favor this day. May the God of your salvation reveal Himself to you in a great and mighty way as your spirit opens up and sees the inheritance that you have. The hope to which you have been called and the glorious power that rose Jesus from the dead that is dwelling in you as He has seated you above all wickedness, all rule, and authority, at the right hand of God with Christ Jesus. Heirs of God, and co-heirs of Jesus. Thank you, Father. He keeps saying to me, "Keep drinking of Me from the wells of salvation." The Lord finds you irresistible, and He loves you. He wants you to know that He loves you.

THE NOTES OF A WARRIOR

CHAPTER 6

The Middleman

"Therefore, brethren, having boldness to enter the Holiest by the blood of Jesus, by a new and living way which He consecrated for us, through the veil, that is, His flesh," Hebrews 10:19-20

DISCUSSION:

I am released to tell you something that I never thought I would share. I am letting you know that there is so much that you will never know. You cannot exhaust the knowledge of God. You cannot go to the bottom of it. In eternity you will be continually learning but never getting to the end of it, ever. God is ever increasing, your learning will ever increase, but you will never come to the end of understanding. I never heard this ever being spoken of before. Most people will not receive the truth. You think you want the truth, but then when you start to get into it, you realize that it does not fit your agenda. Then if you do not adjust, you become hard, and it's what happens in every generation. People become hard, and then they are not usable because they are not changeable. Your ideas are wrong until you have an encounter with Jesus Christ and with the Holy Spirit. You need to change, and once you meet Him, you either harden or you soften, but there is no middle ground. Unfortunately, people are not approaching the Gospel this way. Jesus did when He gave us the parable of the sower in Matthew 13. This parable is not the parable of the sower; Jesus told me it is the parable of the *soils*. This parable is talking about the soils, which are men's hearts. Only one sentence apiece is used to describe the sower and the seed. Yet we emphasize the seed and the sower, and we use it to talk about money, but it is not talking about money. The sower sows the Word. Money and prosperity are part of the Gospel, of course, but some people do not accept that either. If you are going to get all that Jesus said, you have to accept it literally.

- ❖ **Matthew 13:3-9** NLT "He told many stories in the form of parables, such as this one: 'Listen! A farmer went out to plant some seeds. As he scattered them across his field, some seeds fell on a footpath, and the birds came and ate them. Other seeds fell on shallow soil with underlying rock. The seeds sprouted quickly because the soil was shallow. But the plants soon wilted under the hot sun, and since they didn't have deep roots, they died. Other seeds fell among thorns that grew up and choked out the tender plants. Still other seeds fell on fertile soil, and they produced a crop that was thirty, sixty, and even a hundred times as much as had been planted! Anyone with ears to hear should listen and understand.'"

    - Jesus here is speaking about the four types of soils which represent the four conditions of men's hearts. Each condition equals 25 percent.
    - Out of the four, only one condition of the heart produces a crop.
    - That means that you have only a 25 percent chance of receiving a crop when the Word is sown. The Word is the seed.
    - In a room of 100 people, only 25 are going to understand what I say as I preach when I sow the Word of God to produce a crop.
    - Out of those 25 people with good soil (good hearts), eight will produce a 30-fold increase, eight will produce a 60-fold increase, and *only* eight are going to have the hundredfold return. If you divide 25 by three, you get around eight each.
    - That means that when I preach the Gospel in a room of 100 people, only 25 people are going to have the good soil to receive the seed.
    - Only eight people in a room of 100 will receive a hundredfold return.
    - That was what Jesus taught.

According to Mathew 13:10-11, why did Jesus say that He spoke in parables? As a born-again Christian, does that include you?

THE NOTES OF A WARRIOR

- ❖ The importance of The Parable about the Sower and the sowing of the Word is about the importance of *the person receiving it*. The most important part is the receiving of the Word, not the giving of the Word.

  - It is a direct violation of God's Kingdom principles to take a whole parable and make it about something that it is not.
  - It is satan's device to manipulate Scripture so that you never get the full truth about anything.
  - satan's device is to make sure that you do not have a proper understanding of what is being spoken.
  - He will not stop it from being spoken, but he twists everything so that when it gets to you, it does not produce a crop in your heart.
  - Of the four types of soil, three of them he had already sabotaged.
  - He had made one person's heart very hard. (The beaten-down soil).
  - He had made another person's heart have thorns in it, which are the cares of this world.
  - He put rocks in one, which is the deceitfulness of riches.
  - So, there was one left, but even out of that good soil, he could control how much you get out of your crop by not allowing you to understand.
  - satan made that parable about money and money is not mentioned.
  - How many times has it been used in an offering teaching?
  - Jesus said this is the deep mysteries of the Kingdom of Heaven.

- ❖ What if you need healing? You see, the Word of God has everything in it that you need, but you should not focus on one thing because you need it all.

The four types of soil in the Parable of the Soils represent men's hearts. What are the four conditions of men's hearts?

_____

_____

_____

_____

- ❖ <u>Matthew 13:10-11</u> "And the disciples came and said to Him, 'Why do You speak to them in parables?' He answered and said to them, 'Because it has been given to you to know the mysteries of the kingdom of heaven, but to them it has not been given.'"

THE MYSTERIES OF THE KINGDOM

- ❖ **Jesus said something in this Scripture in Matthew that is never emphasized. It is the most important part of this parable. He said in principle, "If you understand this parable, you understand the deep mysteries of the Kingdom." Jesus is talking about the Kingdom of Heaven.**

- ❖ The Kingdom of God works a certain way. You were not invited to the meeting when they designed the Kingdom of God. They did it without you.

  - You have no authority to change anything about the way that God operates. Manipulation is out of the question.
  - Control is out of the question on your part. You have no say so.
  - If Christianity were preached this way, it would not be very popular because everybody wants their way.
  - Everybody has their beliefs, and they want their way. If they do not get it, they cry; they throw a tantrum. They control.
  - They pull their money out so that you do not have their money anymore. You know that is what happens in churches.

- If you do not do what the people want, they say, "Well, we are leaving." Well, go ahead, I will even hold the door for you.
- I am not tied to the financial system of the church. I am tied to the financial system of God, which means I am a sent one.

- I am not going to be manipulated by people that say well if you do not do what we say we are pulling our money out, and we are leaving.
- Well, go ahead. How many pastors can do that and not be controlled? I have seen this happen too many times.

❖ <u>**1 Corinthians 2:9-12**</u> "But as it is written: Eye has not seen, nor ear heard, nor have entered into the heart of man the things which God has prepared for those who love Him. But God has revealed *them* to us through His Spirit. For the Spirit searches all things, yes, the deep things of God. For what man knows the things of a man except the spirit of the man which is in him? Even so no one knows the things of God except the Spirit of God. Now we have received, not the spirit of the world, but the Spirit who is from God, that we might know the things that have been freely given to us by God."

- Paul says this, "The Spirit searches the deep things of God," the mysteries.
- It is the same wording that Jesus used in Matthew 13:10-11.
- Paul says here, "Eye has not seen, nor ear heard, nor entered into the heart of man the things God has prepared for those who love Him."
- That is the most quoted section, but Paul goes on: He says, *"But God has revealed them to us by His Spirit."*
- To control you, people will withhold information from you to keep you under their control. They will not let you know everything.

- satan, Hillel, fell when he ate from the tree, and his eyes were opened, and he saw how he could usurp authority and insert himself between God and man.
- He had to gain control of man by causing them to doubt.
- What he did was he inserted in Eve's mind that God was withholding something from them, which He was not.
- God did not make man to function with a choice between good and evil. They were made to only know good.
- If they knew the option of evil, they would not have the power like God does to choose the right thing in any situation.
- We would be seduced and tempted because we are the weaker image of God. We are not God.
- God put that tree in the garden and ate from it in front of them every time He came down to visit them. It is time that people know what is going on.

How has God revealed His secrets to us? What would happen if you did not spend time in the *secret place*? What happens when you do?

_____
_____
_____
_____

SATAN'S PLAN IS FOR YOU TO DOUBT GOD

❖ satan knew that he had to get the perception of man and woman to change and doubt God. He inserted himself between God and man as a middleman and brokered a deal, which is what he still does all the time.

- If you are a real estate agent, but I know the owner of the house, I do not need you. I could go to the owner and buy the house from them.

- However, what happens is that the agents gather enough information and do enough paperwork to make it so complicated that they create a need for themselves. There is nothing wrong with real estate agents.
- What I am trying to tell you is that this is not the Kingdom of God.
- The Kingdom of God does not need to have someone broker a deal except Jesus Christ Himself, which He has already done.
- Jesus has already bridged the gap and brought us together with the Father.
- He said, "You can go to the Father yourself in My name now" (see John 14:13-14).

DISCUSSION:

It is all about inserting yourself into a situation and saying, "I tell you what. I will talk to them, and I will make a deal." I can say, "I do not need you to; I have their number, and I can call Him myself." "But you do not know how to do the paperwork." "Yes, I do. I watched it on *YouTube*." Their face washes out, and they realize that the power is given back to the people through the Gospel. It has also been given back to us through the media, and even YouTube. Now you can tell if your mechanic is lying to you. You can go on Amazon and buy the little device that you can put into your car and tell you what the real problem is. Then you can match it against what the middleman is telling you.

In the garden satan caused Eve to doubt God. When has there been a time in your life that you have doubted God? How would you handle it differently now that you are more aware of the enemy's tactics?

_____
_____
_____
_____

- **Hebrews 10:19-21** "Therefore, brethren, having boldness to enter the Holiest by the blood of Jesus, by a new and living way which He consecrated for us, through the veil, that is, His flesh, and *having* a High Priest over the house of God,"

  - The Holy Spirit was sent to bridge the gap between you and the Father.
  - You do not need to depend upon someone who inserts themselves like a priest who says, "You need to come through me to get to God. You need to confess your sins to me, a priest."
  - No, I do not need to confess my sins to you.
  - I have a new and living way made open to me through Jesus' blood, according to the book of Hebrews (see Hebrews 10:20-22).
  - When Jesus shared the Gospel, He made it so that everyone could come to the Father in His name.
  - Jesus did not insert Himself in there and then have you charged for access.
  - Anyone who has an exclusive corner on the market of a ministry, or anything that has to do with the Gospel, is a middleman and has his own agenda.
  - The agenda of God was to make God accessible through Jesus Christ and His blood without a middleman.
  - Churches, apostles, prophets, pastors, teachers and evangelists who are the governments of God, are given to the body to build them up and strengthen them so that they come into unity.
  - However, if the result is disunity, then something is wrong. It is not the system that God instituted.
  - It means that man has inserted himself as a middleman somehow and is brokering a deal.

THE NOTES OF A WARRIOR

Some people think that they need a middleman between God and themselves. Explain God's agenda and why this is not true.

_____
_____
_____
_____

DISCUSSION:

You have heard of the term red tape. We were newly married, and we had saved enough money to get our own house and have it built. The builders had done something wrong in building it. When I would pray, the Spirit of the Lord would tell me something different than what I was being told to do to correct their mistake. The big corporation that builds these houses and their lawyers are so powerful. They had already determined if anybody gives them trouble that they would make it disappear and squash any voice that speaks against them. Squashing voices is what governments do. I know this, but I wish I did not know because the more that I know, the more righteous indignation comes up in me from the throne. The system is corrupt because people have inserted themselves into the process, and it is called red tape. What the Spirit of the Lord told me to do was find someone who would tell me the truth about the situation that was not involved with the corporation. When I tried to get them to come and correct what they had done wrong, they did not want to tell me the truth because the truth would expose their lie. It is the same as the Kingdom of God. The Kingdom is going to expose lies, falsehood, manipulation, and control. There is a watchdog committee that was formed by the people. It is called the Registrar of Contractors, which is an organization where you can report a contractor that has done something wrong. They will take action on your behalf. They had become so powerful that when I talked to them, they told me exactly what to do to get action. "You file with us, but we will hold it for 30 days," they said. "Here is your file number. Just write the corporation a letter and say you have 30 days to correct this, or we will go to court." I wrote the letter.

Originally it taken six months to get any response from them, but now I got a response within 24 hours after I filed. Within 24 hours, I had the vice president of the corporation that builds the houses (in an Armani suit) at my door. He said to me, "Mr. Zadai, what can we do to make this go away." All of a sudden, I held all the cards. I had exposed the imposter, and when he was found out, he knew he had to repay even though he was not going to repay the day before. It was the fear of being exposed that caused action. He was not sorry for what he had done to hurt a newly married couple that wanted to get their first house. He was not sorry that he got caught; he just wanted it to go away, and so I made him pay. I said, "I want you to turn my backyard into a nice park with fountains and flowers and flagstone." He said, "It is done." He shook my hand and left. He came back and fixed the house and made my backyard a park.

What are the governments of God on the earth? Why are they given to the Body of Christ?

_____

_____

_____

_____

- ❖ **Warrior Note: I want to tell you one of the most important messages you will ever hear; The Holy Spirit is a very aggressive Person.**

    - You have been told He is a gentleman and that He kind of fades back.
    - It is because you have insulted the Holy Spirit that He fades back because He is grieved, but He is not weak (see Ephesians 4:30-32).
    - Look at the way that the Holy Spirit arrived when He was introduced on the day of Pentecost.
    - He was not a nice, kind, little, soft-spoken gentleman from London drinking tea with His pinkie extended, no. **The Holy Spirit was powerful and forceful.**

THE NOTES OF A WARRIOR

How do you grieve the Holy Spirit according to Ephesians 4:30-32?

_____
_____
_____
_____

> ❖ <u>Warrior Note:</u> **This is what I know about the Holy Spirit that I have not been able to release, but I am releasing it now. The Holy Spirit is an Enforcer of the blessing. He is an Enforcer of the truth.**
>
> - He is an Advocate. That is the same word that is used for a lawyer.
> - If you have ever dealt with a lawyer, they say to you, "Tell me everything you know because I do not want to be surprised when I get in the courtroom. I do not want you to say a word unless I tell you to, you let *me* talk." That is like the Holy Spirit.
> - The Holy Spirit knows the truth about everything.

On the day of Pentecost, how did the Holy Spirit introduce Himself in the upper room (see Acts 2:1-4)? How would you describe the Holy Spirit?

_____
_____
_____
_____

CHAPTER 7

The Slanderer

"Then I heard a loud voice saying in heaven, 'Now salvation, and strength, and the kingdom of our God, and the power of His Christ have come, for the accuser of our brethren, who accused them before our God day and night, has been cast down.'" Revelation 12:10

DISCUSSION:

I saw this on the other side and was not able to talk about it until now. The agenda of satan and demons is to know the truth of God. They know the desired result that the Father had when He spoke it. They know God's intent and, if left alone, know that it will accomplish what it was sent to do. They already know the truth about a certain thing. I was shown all this, I was literally there and watched the demons engage in this. The whole idea is not to discredit the truth, and they do not go after the truth. The demons are told to go after *your credibility*. They discredit the receiver. Why is satan called the slanderer? satan cannot dispute absolute truth. He has no power to do that, so he slanders, attacks, and discredits *you*. Jesus told me that the whole purpose of misrepresenting the Parable of the Sower, which is really the Parable of the Soils is to discredit you. To eliminate the possibility of your receiving of it. Or if you have received it to prevent you from producing one hundredfold return.

My classmates in school studied Greek and Hebrew with me. One of my friends is now an authority that sits on a board that determines translations of the Bible. He can do that because he continued with his education. If I had continued, I would have been on the same board in the same position, but I chose not to. What the translators do not tell you is that nobody is an expert on a language except someone brought up in that language from birth. The Hebrew and Greek languages, the ancient ones are dead languages. These are languages that have fallen by the wayside, yet people will claim to be a scholar of them, and some of those people sat in the same classes that I did.

THE AUTHORITY OF THE BIBLE

- ❖ There are usually four different definitions for every word in the Bible, and you can look them up in word studies. They give you a choice and number the definitions one through four. Their number is based on the order of how often they are used in a certain way in the Bible.

    - If you look, some scholars will choose a definition for a word that is rarely used that way because it fits their agenda.
    - What happens if what you think is an authority is really just a middleman?
    - What if I told you that the people King James chose to interpret your Bible were afraid of him because of his perverse sexual preferences. The translators did not translate everything that had to do with sexual preference correctly in the Greek and the Hebrew.
    - What if I told you that they were afraid of losing their heads? Why are some translations a little harder on sexual sins than the King James version?

- ❖ **The translation that is best is the one that displays the power of God, and that is what Jesus told me. If anything takes away from the power of God, it is not the right translation.**

    - A Greek professor told me that the most accurate translation, according to the Greek, is the *Amplified* version.

- Languages that are more colorful are more difficult to translate with accuracy because they are very wordy.
- When Jesus spoke to me, He spoke very colorfully, but I recognized it. Like I would recognize the *King James* version except for the "thee's" and "thou's."
- When Jesus spoke, there were more of what you would call adjectives, and it was more descriptive, wordier.
- Jesus spoke to me in a language called Aramaic, which on earth was His native language at the time.

Why are some translations of the Bible more accurate than others? How can you tell which translation is the best?

_____
_____
_____
_____

- ❖ I am a Doctor of Theology. I have authority, and I am exposing the fact that you have placed authority in certain people, and they do not have the authority.

  - There are certain people that do not want you to know certain things because if you know these things, then the lie will be exposed, and they will not have control over you.
  - In court, if you withhold information, it is just the same as lying.
  - satan wants to withhold information so he can twist the information he does give to you.
  - The vilest thing that we have to deal with on this earth is deception.

❖ I can tell you certain things and use certain definitions that *are* there but skew or misinform you in a nice way. I can tell you nicely that I have your best interests at heart, but it is a lie.

- The demons have already determined the truth, but they do not want *you* to know the truth.
- satan knows the truth about a certain subject beforehand. He has determined that his demons are not going to challenge that truth. Instead, they are going to go after the receiver and discredit them.
- satan tells his demons to keep people from the truth and to tell people how concerned they are about them, and how much they care about them, but they do not.
- Under the auspices of telling someone, "We care about you," the whole time, demons know exactly what the truth is. And they are going to keep you from it. satan does not want you to know the truth.
- Not that you want to do this, but if you pulled aside every demon and interviewed them, you would find that they are instructed to keep people away from the absolute truth that was established in Heaven.

Demons know the truth, but why are they trying to keep *you* from knowing the truth (see John 8:32)?

_____
_____
_____
_____

❖ **Warrior Note: satan knows what God has spoken over you. More importantly, he does not want you to know the full power and revelation of that Word. That is why we have so many translations of the Bible. That is why you do not know who you are for years when you should know immediately.**

- Do not wait for years to know what your purpose is in Christ
- These demons are instructed to twist everything.
- They make you think that you are outside looking in, but you are really inside, making faces at them because they are out.
- The switch has to happen in you.
- **You have to be empowered by revelation.**

Why is satan afraid of you knowing the full power and revelation of what God has spoken over you? How can you make sure that you know?

_____
_____
_____
_____

- ❖ <u>Matthew 12:32</u> "Anyone who speaks a word against the Son of Man, it will be forgiven him; but whoever speaks against the Holy Spirit, it will not be forgiven him, either in this age or in the *age* to come."

  - The most misunderstood individual in the Trinity is the Holy Spirit.
  - The most discredited person is the Holy Spirit.
  - Jesus said, "If you speak against the Holy Spirit, it will not be forgiven in this life or in the next."
  - Why did Jesus say that? It was because we do not understand who the Holy Spirit is. You cannot violate Him.
  - No one has ever told you these things because it is kept from you.
  - Ministers do not pay the price on knowing Him.
  - The Ministers who do dedicate their whole life to knowing the Holy Spirit get hit and disappear.

What happens when someone speaks a word against the Holy Spirit?

_____
_____
_____
_____

- ❖ If they would let me on Christian TV and talk about this, then everyone would be informed, and they would get rid of this middleman.

  - This process of having individuals inserted into your life that you have to go through keeps the body of Christ uninformed.
  - The Five-Fold Ministry of the church has been given to us to build us up and to unify us.
  - If that is not happening, then it is not God's fault. People do not want to be controlled because the Spirit is the Spirit of liberty.
  - The Spirit of God will not allow you to feel comfortable being manipulated or controlled.
  - There are evil spirits that perform miracles through ministers. Some have made covenants with evil spirits. I know this, and it is not hearsay.

DECEPTION

- ❖ <u>Matthew 24:37</u> "But as the days of Noah *were,* so also will the coming of the Son of Man be."

- ❖ <u>Matthew 24:24</u> "For false christs and false prophets will rise and show great signs and wonders to deceive, if possible, even the elect."

- This Scripture in Matthew warns us that there are going to be lying signs and wonders performed and that the very elect would be deceived if that were even possible. Jesus Himself said this.
- There is disinformation that causes the truth to be undermined.
- You are fed information that causes a wrong perception, and you never receive the truth.
- You accept something from an authority that is really not an authority.

How can you prevent yourself from being deceived? Where does absolute truth come from?

_____
_____
_____
_____

- ❖ satan was in a snake. The Lord God Jehovah came down every day and talked to Adam and Eve in the garden and walked with them (see Genesis 3:8).
    - Eve could have asked God anything she wanted, and He would have told her. Why was she talking to a snake about doctrinal truth (see Genesis 3:1-5)? Why did Eve get into that conversation?
    - lucifer had fallen and was inserting himself as a middleman.
    - He was feeding Adam and Eve information knowing the truth, with the goal that *they* would never know the truth.
    - satan was going to discredit them, so in essence he said, "You know God knows that if you eat of this tree, you are going to be like Him."
    - They already were like Him. If they ate of the tree, they would no longer be like Him because they could not handle knowing evil.
    - God ate from that tree every day in front of them all and said, "Do not eat of this tree." That was to remind them of who God is.
    - Now here is the thing no one has ever said. I saw that we were so much like God that we would actually think we were God.

- God did not *need* to put this tree in the garden; He *had* to put that in the garden to remind us that even though we are like Him we are *not* Him. Left to ourselves, we would think that we are gods.
- Even Jesus said to the Pharisees, "Is it not written in your law, 'I said, "You are gods."' If He called them gods to whom the Word of God came" (John 10:34).
- The word "gods" is also used to mean "a judge," Jesus said, "Because it is written, it cannot be revoked" (see John 10:35).

❖ **2 Timothy 3:7** "always learning and never able to come to the knowledge of the truth."

- I wanted to show you how the demons have discussed the strategy on how you will never come to the truth.
- Always searching for it but never obtaining it.

If someone is always learning and never coming to the knowledge of the truth, what are they missing? What advice would you give them?

_____
_____
_____
_____

REVELATION THROUGH THE HOLY SPIRIT

❖ **1 Corinthians 2:10** "But God has revealed *them* to us through His Spirit. For the Spirit searches all things, yes, the deep things of God."

- God has revealed these deep mysteries to us by His Spirit.

- To show you how demons work, most Ministers quote 1 Corinthians 2:9. "Eye has not seen, nor ear heard, nor have entered into the heart of man the things which God has prepared for those who love Him."
- Everybody quotes this verse, but the conclusion is in 2:10, and you must read through. It says, "It has been revealed through His Spirit.
- These verses in 1 Corinthians 2:11-16 go on and talk about how a spiritual person can receive spiritual things, but a carnal person cannot.
- A carnal person cannot judge a spiritual person because they do not have the authority.
- We cannot be judged by the people of the world because they are carnal.
- Only a spiritual Christian can judge you.
- At the end of all this in verse 2:16, Paul says, "But we have the mind of Christ."
- Paul would show a dilemma, and he knew how to speak. He would build a case against us, and then he would give us the solution.
- The solution would be Christ Jesus.

Why is it that only a spiritual Christian can judge you? Why is it that a carnal person cannot judge you?

___
___
___
___

Romans 7:19-20 "For the good that I will *to do,* I do not do; but the evil I will not *to do,* that I practice. Now if I do what I will not *to do,* it is no longer I who do it, but sin that dwells in me."

Romans 7:24-25 "O wretched man that I am! Who will deliver me from this body of death? I thank God—through Jesus Christ our Lord. So then, with the mind I myself serve the law of God, but with the flesh the law of sin."

Romans 8:1-2 *"There is* therefore now no condemnation to those who are in Christ Jesus, who do not walk according to the flesh, but according to the Spirit. For the law of the Spirit of life in Christ Jesus has made me free from the law of sin and death."

Romans 8:7-8 "Because the carnal mind *is* enmity against God; for it is not subject to the law of God, nor indeed can be. So then, those who are in the flesh cannot please God."

- ❖ If you read Paul's writings, he is building a case in Romans 7. He begins by talking about how the good that he wants to do; he does not do. The evil he does not want to do; he does.

    - Paul then talks about how wretched he is and what help does he have.
    - Who will deliver him?
    - He thanks God–through Christ Jesus, our Lord.
    - There is now no condemning voice and no case against us.
    - It has been canceled through Jesus Christ.
    - The condemning voice has been canceled for those who do not walk according to the flesh but according to the Spirit.
    - Those who yield to the flesh cannot please God, and they are enemies of God. It is impossible for them to please God.
    - There is a direct war against the Spirit and the flesh, and they are enemies of each other, and that is never quoted.

❖ **Can you see that when people tell you things, they are not telling you the absolute truth because it is being kept from you? The people keeping information from you might be doing it because they have a selfish agenda. Or they might want to create a place for themselves as a middleman so that they are asked back to your church because you need them.**

CHAPTER 8

Centurion Faith

"The centurion answered and said, "Lord, I am not worthy that You should come under my roof. But only speak a word, and my servant will be healed."
Matthew 8:8

DISCUSSION:

Jesus commended the Centurion. He had great faith because he did not need Jesus to come to his house and lay hands on his servant who was paralyzed. He said, "Only speak a word, and my servant will be healed." "When Jesus heard it, He marveled, and said to those who followed, 'Assuredly, I say to you, I have not found such great faith, not even in Israel'" (see Matthew 8:10). You can understand why I do not want to lay hands on people because I want you to go to Centurion faith, "Kevin, just speak the word over me, speak a blessing over us and then let us go to our cars." That is great faith, and that was Jesus' goal. Jesus marveled at that man. That man did not need Jesus to even go to his home. For instance, when you have fire tunnels in church, it can become a circus. After a while it becomes a mode of operation. I do not wear contacts anymore. I received my healing sitting in a chair in my office when the glory of God came in, and I had a visitation. There were no TV cameras, there were no witnesses, there was no offering taken, no one breathed on me, and no one waved their jacket over me. I did not feel any hands on me and yet I was healed. I had to start wearing contacts in 1983. I believed God every day since 1983 the whole way until 2018. Yet, I received my healing, and I was not in church, and I was not giving an offering of a thousand dollars. The mode of operation for healing is based on established truth from Heaven, the way the Kingdom of God works. You receive a hundredfold return on the seed that is sown into *you*, not the seed that you sow into *someone else*. Did you see how it is all twisted? The Parable of the Soils is talking about you being a good receiver. When did it become about pushing you to give? satan knows when. Jesus is basically saying in the parable of the Soils, "Hey listen if you get this parable you understand the whole kingdom." When satan heard that we could understand the whole kingdom, he realized that he had to discredit the whole idea. What satan planned to do is discredit the receiver and make him believe the parable was about giving. The whole time, you have got problems with your soil; your heart issues, and no one is helping you with that. You are hoping that it gets better tomorrow, but you are still hurting inside. You continue to hurt every day, and you go to service after service buying DVD's, books, and watching Christian television.

- ❖ **Hebrews 11:17-19** "By faith Abraham, when he was tested, offered up Isaac, and he who had received the promises offered up his only begotten *son,* of whom it was said, "In Isaac your seed shall be called," concluding that God *was* able to raise *him* up, even from the dead, from which he also received him in a figurative sense."

    - Abraham was told to take his son up and offer him, but Abraham did not expect to kill him.
    - He was going to offer up his son (see Genesis 22:1-19).
    - Abraham went all the way with it knowing that God would stop him. Why? Because God had already told him that, "Through Isaac your seed shall be called."
    - *This is Centurion faith because* God spoke it, and that was enough.
    - Abraham waited all that time until he could not have children and then had one. He knew that God would not lie.
    - That is where you have to allow your discernment to kick in, where you know that God is not going to lie to you.
    - You have got to accept that.

THE NOTES OF A WARRIOR

Why did Abraham trust that God would not let him offer up his son Isaac? What are you trusting God for in your life?

_____
_____
_____
_____

- ❖ **Romans 3:3-4** "For what if some did not believe? Will their unbelief make the faithfulness of God without effect? Certainly not! Indeed, let God be true but every man a liar."

- ❖ **Numbers 23:19** "God *is* not a man, that He should lie, Nor a son of man, that He should repent. Has He said, and will He not do? Or has He spoken, and will He not make it good?"

  - God is not a liar. That is absolute truth.
  - When it comes down to it, no one is going to testify of God's unfaithfulness in Heaven.
  - No one is going to approach God and say He was unfaithful.
  - There is no one that is going to tell God that He lied.
  - Because of the characteristics and personality of God, the only way that satan can get to you is to discredit.
  - satan makes you think, "These people have my concern. They want to help me," but they do not, they have an agenda.
  - From now on, your discernment is going to have to be through the roof.
  - To have discernment, you do not have to stay up all night fasting, praying, and studying. You just have to accept absolute truth.

- ❖ **Psalm 89:14** "Righteousness and justice *are* the foundation of Your throne; Mercy and truth go before Your face."

- There are layers to God's throne. The foundation of His throne is righteousness and justice. Mercy and truth go before Him.
- His faithfulness surrounds Him (see Psalm 89:8). In a previous verse it refers to the Angels as being that entourage of faithfulness.
- God's throne is established, and He sits on these foundations with different beautiful gemstones, and they have names on them.
- When God talks to you, He is talking from a platform that is irrevocable. You think, "I do not hear anybody talking like this."
- *God is the authority*, and He sets in the church some to be apostles, prophets, pastors, teachers, and evangelists. This Five-Fold Ministry God has instituted in the church.
- The Spirit of God works all things as *He* wills, not *you* will or as an apostle wills, but as the Spirit wills. Individually He is giving you gifts according to Paul (see 1 Corinthians 12:11).

Describe the foundation of God's throne, and what goes before Him? How does knowing that impact your life?

_____
_____
_____
_____

❖ <u>2 Corinthians 9:5-7</u> "Therefore I thought it necessary to exhort the brethren to go to you ahead of time, and prepare your generous gift beforehand, which *you had* previously promised, that it may be ready as *a matter of* generosity and not as a grudging obligation. But this *I say:* He who sows sparingly will also reap sparingly, and he who sows bountifully will also reap bountifully. *So let* each one *give* as he purposes in his heart, not grudgingly or of necessity; for God loves a cheerful giver."

- In this passage, Paul is giving a proper teaching on giving.
- That is not in the Parable of the Soils, which is about men's hearts.
- I use this as an example to show you that satan wants to discredit.
- He will not confront truth, but what he will do is shift your perception and keep you from the *power* of the truth.
- The enemy wants you to never come to the truth, but always be seeking it.

THE TRUTH DWELLS IN YOU

❖ **John 14:6** "Jesus said to him, 'I am the way, the truth, and the life. No one comes to the Father except through Me.'"

DISCUSSION:

I was in a small town in Italy. The person who invited me there was seated with my wife and me. I looked out the door, and Jesus was there standing looking at me. He wanted to talk to me. He has done this a number of times to me. I left the table, and Jesus began to brief me on instructions for my missions trip. Later in the trip, we were in another city, and had a big seminar, and many people came. I got up to speak, and there were two young boys on the second row, just sitting there smiling. The Lord spoke to me and said, "So that you know, all the finances that come in for these two weeks will be going to them." Now, after reading what the Lord told me, do you still want to be a minister? Our life is not our own. I stopped speaking even though I just started. I went over to the man in charge, and whispered, "So you know, do not cut the check to me. Cut the check to these two guys and split it between them. He asked, "Why?" I said, "Because those two, when they grow up are going to go from the south to the north as evangelists through this country. I want to be in on the bottom level of what God is doing in their lives." He had to talk to them in Italian to tell them. The one boy called his dad that night at the Vatican who was the head of the Charismatic Renewal for the Catholic Church, answering only to the Pope. He said, "Dad you have got to meet Kevin Zadai," and so we did. We went to his house and had dinner and ate real spaghetti with real meatballs! His dad sat there in tears, and he said to me, "Any door you want in the world is open to you." I did not take him up on it because God did not tell me to do that.

Understand that the truth dwells in you, it is who you are, and it becomes you. The truth opens doors because of who you are. You are an obedient servant, you obey everything, and Jesus visits you. He orchestrates everything in your life. I got to meet someone that I would never have met, and this is absolute truth, and it is how every believer is supposed to operate. My wife and I cannot take any credit for any of this. The Jesus I met has given us great authority on the earth if we are under Him. However, I cannot let anyone discredit what God is saying or even discredit me.

What happens when the truth dwells in you? As a believer, how should you be operating?

_____
_____
_____
_____

- ❖ Why are people being riled up about healing? Why are they riled up about the Holy Spirit and speaking in tongues? Why is it so controversial?

    - Why is it so controversial to pray for the sick or to tell people they need to speak in tongues, or they need to be baptized in the Holy Spirit?
    - The reason is that satan knows that if you in any way allow the Word to take root in your heart that the crop will be a hundredfold, and then there is nothing he can do to stop it.
    - You are going to propagate the kingdom everywhere you go, not because of what you say but because of *who you are.*
    - People will see the fruit of your life, and they will want that.

THE NOTES OF A WARRIOR

Why are people riled up about healing, speaking in tongues, and the baptism of the Holy Spirit? Who are you in Christ Jesus?

_____

_____

_____

_____

- ❖ People will ask, "You are 94 years old, but you look like you are 30, what are you doing?" You tell them, "I take this supplement." Everybody you meet is going to want to buy that supplement right away, because of the fruit. Right?

    - Everybody is into their diets. "How did you lose 100 pounds?" "I am on this diet." Everybody wants that diet right. It is because you can see the results.
    - The disinformation campaign that satan and these demons have is that they want to discredit because they know that the fruit that will be produced in your life. If you understand the Parable of the Soils, it is dangerous to them.
    - satan and his demons know that if the idea of the whole parable takes root in you, and that Word takes effect, that the fruit produced in that crop will be a hundredfold.
    - Then there would be nothing that satan or those evil spirits could do to stop it from propagating. You will distribute it everywhere you go.

What is the fruit of the Gospel that people can see in your life? How can you increase the fruit in your life?

_____

_____

_____

_____

There has to come this time where truth overthrows lies. The experience that you go through is not the truth.

- Your experience is facts, and it does not interpret correctly the personality of God all the time because we live in a broken world.
- You cannot draw conclusions about your relationship with God by how people treat you or how you felt this morning before you got to the coffeemaker.
- You cannot interpret your relationship with God based on circumstances. You must *tell* your circumstances *who God is*.

❖ <u>**John 1:12**</u> "But as many as received Him, to them He gave the right to become children of God, to those who believe in His name: who were born, not of blood, nor of the will of the flesh, nor of the will of man, but of God."

- The circumstances need to be told of who God is and that you have been sent.
- That as a child of God, you have been given authority to become a child of God.
- The Holy Spirit is inside of you to enforce the blessing. The angels are on the outside of you to enforce the blessing.
- The demons do not have a chance if you adopt truth because the Holy Spirit will engage you on the inside and the angels will engage you on the outside.
- You will be escorted into truth, which is the blessing. God only has a two-item menu. He said, "Choose you this day." Do you want a blessing or a cursing (see Deuteronomy 28)?
- God only gave them two choices. You go to most restaurants, and you have a catalog full of choices.
- With God, it is, "Do you choose to obey Me and serve Me and live by the truth or do you want to live by the lie."

- Those who have given themselves up to the lie it says are deceived, and they are reprobate.

- ❖ **Romans 1:25** "who exchanged the truth of God for the lie and worshiped and served the creature rather than the Creator, who is blessed forever. Amen."

  - They have handed themselves over, and they believed the lie. The deceived does not adhere to the truth.
  - Jesus was revolutionary because He was not giving His opinion, and the Pharisees were all about opinion. The Pharisees were all about control, and they wanted to keep the people out.

- ❖ **Now *you* have become a target to be discredited because you have the truth.**

  - Now satan attacks *you* and tells you that you are not worthy. He tells you that you have blown it. And that you will never amount to anything, and he even gets your parents to tell you that when growing up.
  - When my dad became a Christian, he started crying because he realized that he was not speaking by the Spirit of God or an angel; he was speaking by an evil spirit.
  - He apologized in tears for cursing me all my life. He said, "I did not know, you were my first son, and I just did what my dad did."
  - The point is that satan will come at you and discredit you, so you do not receive what is given to you fully by your loving Heavenly Father.
  - Never forget this message—Never, ever doubt what God has for you. Never doubt that you are worthy because you are? Never doubt it.
  - Jesus has pronounced you worthy because He gave Himself for you. And because He offered Himself up for you, you have *everything*.
  - satan does not want you to know this.

How does satan try to discredit people today even though the Word of God is so readily available? How can you overcome his tactics?

_____
_____
_____
_____

- ❖ Every one of you has been told who the devil is.

  - However, he is not what you think he is. He was nothing close.
  - When I met Jesus, he was not like what I was told. He was so much more.
  - lucifer is a beautiful being. He is not red, and he does not have horns. He does not have a pitchfork, and he is not stupid.

- ❖ **Ezekiel 28:12-15** "Thus says the Lord GOD: 'You *were* the seal of perfection, full of wisdom and perfect in beauty. You were in Eden, the garden of God; Every precious stone *was* your covering: The sardius, topaz, and diamond, beryl, onyx, and jasper, sapphire, turquoise, and emerald with gold. The workmanship of your timbrels and pipes was prepared for you on the day you were created. You *were* the anointed cherub who covers; I established you; You were on the holy mountain of God; You walked back and forth in the midst of fiery stones. You *were* perfect in your ways from the day you were created, till iniquity was found in you.'"

  - In Ezekiel, it says that lucifer was beautiful, and the seal of perfection. The epitome, the top sum of perfection.
  - He was the sum; he was the example. He was the sum of beauty and perfection until iniquity was found in him, and he fell.
  - We are dealing with someone who actually believes he is God.

- satan absolutely believes that he can take God. He is going to do it by stealing humanity, God's perfection in His image. satan is going to take them away and hold them hostage.

❖ I became a Christian and have been sent to tell everyone that the captives are free. I tell them that their jail cell is unlocked and to come on out. I tell people you can be healed, you can be delivered, you can prosper, and you can be blessed.

- Now you can understand why satan would not want anyone to speak these things. That is why they killed Jesus.
- Jesus went into the ministry at 30, and at 33 and a half years old, they killed him. He lasted three and a half years doing the will of the Father. That is how potent the message is.
- Why do you take it personally when you go through hardship? You have to realize you are on the right track when that happens.

❖ **Psalm 37:5-6** NLT "Commit everything you do to the LORD. Trust him, and he will help you. He will make your innocence radiate like the dawn, and the justice of your cause will shine like the noonday sun."

❖ **Jeremiah 29:11** "For I know the thoughts that I think toward you, says the LORD, thoughts of peace and not of evil, to give you a future and a hope."

❖ The goal of God is to have disciples, to propagate, expand and increase. Everything about God is to increase and to have His family back. The whole thing about redemption is that we were always God's, and God was stolen from, and He wants justice.

- My name Zadai is from *tzedek*, which in Hebrew is the word for righteousness or justice. And I have always had this thing about me that wanted justice.
- And you should never be limited by money in doing what God has asked you to do. There are thousands of ways for God to get money to you.
- We focus on one or two things, and the whole time there is hidden treasure waiting with your name on it. God designated it, and the angels are the ones who know where it is.
- You let the Angels be released in your life to bring forth the wealth, so you can accomplish what God has called you to do.

❖ **Romans 10:17** "So then faith *comes* by hearing, and hearing by the word of God."

- What good is it if people do not hear? What good is truth if they do not hear it, people have to be sent to speak the truth.
- Once you hear the Word, it produces faith.
- Jesus said to "Pray for the Lord of the harvest to send out laborers into His harvest" (Matthew 9:38). Would you pray?
- satan cannot stop people from going if they decide to obey God.
- He can try to stop them, and with some of them he succeeds.
- If he cannot stop them by discrediting them, then he will cut off the supply.
- When I was in Heaven, I saw that no one should ever be limited by money.
- You are not supposed to make your decisions based on money. You are supposed to make your decisions based on the voice of God speaking to you.

- ❖ **Acts 10:38** "how God anointed Jesus of Nazareth with the Holy Spirit and with power, who went about doing good and healing all who were oppressed by the devil, for God was with Him."

  - Jesus went around doing good. What is good? Good is healing all those who are oppressed by the devil.
  - Jesus went around doing good and healing everyone oppressed by the devil. Who is doing the oppressing? The devil.
  - Many people have heard someone interpret this Scripture and say that the reason you did not get healed is that God is trying to teach you something.
  - Then why do you go to the doctor to get out of God's will?
  - If money is evil, why do you sell yourself to your job? Why do you give a corporation eight hours or more of your day?
  - "I do not believe in that prosperity stuff." Then why do you work? "Well, I got to pay my bills." Listen to yourself talk.
  - God said you that you have two choices: the head or the tail; above or beneath; borrower or lender (see Deuteronomy 28:13).

- **John 9:2-3** "And His disciples asked Him, saying, 'Rabbi, who sinned, this man or his parents, that he was born blind?' Jesus answered, 'Neither this man nor his parents sinned, but that the works of God should be revealed in him.'"

  - We will argue about things, but Jesus *was not* sent back to *work against* the Father.
  - If God was making people sick, what sins did this family commit that this person was born blind or born lame? Jesus says neither it was so that God's power could be revealed.
  - Then people take that and say God made him sick so that Jesus could heal him. No, that is not what Jesus was saying.

- ❖ The plan of satan is not to ever allow you to come to the absolute truth about anything. His plan for you is that you always have questions when you should have answers. People are looking for fruit in your life, and they are looking for answers from you.

  - Jesus had answers for everyone. He did not say, "I have got to study, or I have got to go find out, or I don't know." He has the answer.
  - Luke 11:11-12 says, "Do not worry about how or what you are going to say when you are brought before the courts. The Holy Spirit will teach you what you are to say."
  - You need to rely on the Holy Spirit. Just remember that the Holy Spirit is truth. If you yell out *truth,* the Holy Spirit is going to turn and say, "You called?"
  - When you yell out *faithful* Jesus turns on His white horse and says, "What do you want? That is who He is as a person He is faithful (see Revelation 19:11).
  - The Person of the Holy Spirit is inside of you and is going to correct your life from this time forth.
  - The Spirit of God is correcting your path right now.

How does the enemy's plans for you contrast with God's will for your life?

_____
_____
_____
_____

- ❖ In your world right now, you have an opportunity to do more than Jesus had at the time that He lived.

- The world needs to stop and think about the time that we live in.
- We communicate at the speed of light we travel at the speed of sound, and we can alter our genetics with science.
- Only two hundred years ago, our first president George Washington was still on horseback. He communicated by written letter. The culture at the time was agrarian.
- In two hundred and fifty years, look at what has happened.
- It has flipped in our favor. The Gospel can go everywhere.
- That is how I can tell you that we are close to the end. The Gospel is being preached all over the world.
- You need to be healed. You need to be delivered. Then you need to turn and help others to get their soil (their hearts) ready for the Word of God to be placed inside of them and produce a crop.

CHAPTER 9

The Counsel of God

"The counsel of the LORD stands forever, The plans of His heart to all generations." Psalm 33:11

DISCUSSION:

One thing about Jesus, the Son of God, is He came to change you. That word change is transformation. That means that you are not the same when you become born again. When you are born again, you are transformed. The old has passed away, and all things become new (see 2 Corinthians 5:17). I do not think that Christians have grasped this verse yet because old things are gone and behold *everything*—all things—are made new. It actually says that you are a new species that has never existed before, and that is what the phrase, "a new creature in Christ" means. Let that sink in. Jesus did not come only to tell you that you are forgiven, but that there is a transformation. In Romans 7:15, the Apostle Paul talks about how hard it is to keep the law. He said that what he wants to do, he does not do. What he does not want to do that he finds himself doing. In one chapter more Romans 8:1 Paul says, "Thanks be to God through Jesus Christ. There is therefore now no condemnation." In Aramaic, it says, "The case is closed. There is no accusing voice against you in the courts of law."

❖ <u>2 Timothy 2:3-4</u> "You therefore must endure hardship, as a good soldier of Jesus Christ. No one engaged in warfare entangles himself with the affairs of *this* life, that he may please him who enlisted him as a soldier."

- Did Paul the Apostle say that a Christian was a soldier? Why?

- Soldiers provide protection, order, and safety.
- Paul, who was training Timothy, said to him, "*No* man, that warreth entangles himself with the affairs of this life." No exceptions.
- Why? That he may please Him, who chose him to be a soldier.
- Another translation, "Soldiers do not get tied up in civilian affairs."
- Soldiers are enlisted, they are wrapped up in their position, and they listen to their commander. They want to please their commander, and they are not tied up in the affairs of this life.
- In America, we call it drama. There is no drama in a soldier's life, just the facts.
- You are not supposed to get tied up, but caught up in the very Counsel of God.

Are you entangled in the affairs of this life? How can you become a good soldier for Christ?

_____
_____
_____
_____

- **Hebrews 11:5** "By faith Enoch was taken away so that he did not see death, "and was not found, because God had taken him"; for before he was taken he had this testimony, that he pleased God."

    - Are you tied up, or are you caught up?
    - Are you tied up in the affairs of this life, or are you caught up in the Counsel of God?
    - Are you a soldier, or are you a civilian? Paul said we are soldiers.

- There has to come this point in your life where you realize you have been chosen.
- It is interesting to me that Jesus has come and caught me up into His counsel, and I got to meet somebody that was caught up, Enoch.
- I watched Enoch take his last step on this earth. He pleased God so much that God took him.
- Enoch was caught up, he is gone, and he is in Heaven right now.
- It is known that he had pleased God.
- Are you tied up or you caught up? You are going to find out.
- I want to tell you something, the devil fears you.

❖ <u>Warrior Note:</u> **Warriors are not tied up; they are caught up. If you want to be a warrior, and if you want to have special assignments by the Spirit of God, then you need to get caught up in the Counsel of God.**

- God loved Enoch so much that he became irresistible to God. God said, "I have got to have you with Me."
- So, God did not let Enoch go home that night.
- John on the Isle of Patmos was caught up.
- He wrote the Book of Revelation. The Spirit of God came and wrapped him up and took him up to Heaven.
- When you read the Book of Revelation, it is amazing what John saw.

❖ <u>Warrior Note:</u> **The mindset of a warrior is only on one thing. He wants to please his commander.**

- A soldier knows that his commander is not interested in his opinion.
- A soldier is trained to say, "Yes sir," and start doing what he is asked to do before the commander's finish telling him. There is no hesitation.

- The soldier knows his commander's voice.
- He is *fully submitted* and convinced of his commander's authority.
- When the commander speaks, the soldier starts doing what he said immediately.
- The soldier does not have an opinion.
- When God spoke His Word from His throne, He did all this without even inviting you to a meeting.
- You were not invited.
- He wrote a book about your life as it says in Psalms 139:16.
- He wrote it before you were born.
- Why weren't you invited to that meeting? It is because your opinion does not count.
- **Warrior Note: It is called absolute authority**.

How can you please God? Are you tied up or caught up? How can you become fully submitted to God?

_____
_____
_____
_____

- Isaiah 55:11 "So shall My word be that goes forth from My mouth; It shall not return to Me void, but it shall accomplish what I please, and it shall prosper *in the thing* for which I sent it."

THE NOTES OF A WARRIOR

DISCUSSION:

God looks at you, and He thinks you are beautiful. He does not care about your opinion. He does not ask you for your opinion. You look at your flaws, but He looks at your strong points. God remembers the day that He thought of you and spoke you into your mother's womb. He never asked you to attend the meeting when He designed you, and no one voted on it. The Trinity all agreed. The Word of God was spoken from the throne of God. His Word will go out and come back around and accomplish what it said it would do. The Lord expects it, and part of what He spoke out of His mouth was *you*. You will go out and live your life and come back and stand on the spot that God spoke you from in Heaven. That is the absolute truth. You will give an account of your life, and it does not matter what you feel, it is what you know.

- ❖ The reason you go to a counselor is that you need to know something you do not know. You need someone to talk to you who knows what is going on. That is why you seek counsel because you cannot do everything yourself.

    - God in Heaven is waiting, and He is asking you to come and sit with Him.
    - Are you tied up, or are you caught up?
    - **<u>Warrior Note:</u> A soldier focuses on his commander. He focuses on what is said. He is not concerned about the affairs of this life.**
    - When I was with Jesus, His personality was so strong. He cannot understand why people doubt Him.
    - Jesus wept with me when He told me what He did for all the people. He said the people do not know what I have done for them.
    - He wished that people would know the depth of what He went through to completely purchase humanity.
    - When Jesus purchased you, it was not so you would encounter Romans Chapter 7, but so you would encounter Romans Chapter 8.

- In Romans Chapter 8, it finishes with this; "If God is for us who can be against us?"
- Jesus did all of this for us.

Why shouldn't you be living out of Romans chapter seven? Why *should* you be living out of Romans chapter eight?

_____
_____
_____
_____

❖ Your Commander has given some commands out. He is asking you, "Where are your enemies. Just a minute ago, you had a bunch of enemies. What you did not notice is that when Jesus showed up, they showed themselves out.

- They are outnumbered now.
- It is so important to submit to your commander Jesus.
- "Greater is He that is within you than he that is in the world" (1 John 4:4). The Spirit of God wants to convince you.
- It is the Spirit of liberty that I am speaking about. The Son has set you free, and He wants you to be fully convinced.
- He wants you to be caught up in His counsel.

❖ **Psalm 8:4-5** "What is man that You are mindful of him, and the son of man that You visit him? For You have made him a little lower than the angels, and You have crowned him with glory and honor."

❖ **Genesis 1:26** "Then God said, "Let Us make man in Our image, according to Our likeness; let them have dominion over the fish of the sea, over the birds of the air, and over the cattle, over all the earth and over every creeping thing that creeps on the earth."

- God made man in His image. That means that you look like God.
- When the Son of God is revealed, according to Paul, it says we are going to see Him as He is.
- And we will be like Him, and that word is "likeness" is the same as image. You look like Jesus.
- I saw many things when I was in Heaven, but what shocked me the most was that I looked like Him.

❖ **2 Peter 1:4** "by which have been given to us exceedingly great and precious promises, that through these you may be partakers of the divine nature, having escaped the corruption *that is* in the world through lust."

- Peter said all these precious promises have been given to us.
- Through these promises, we can be partakers of the divine nature.
- Peter said that you can escape the corruption that is in the world.

❖ **John 10:34** "Jesus answered them, 'Is it not written in your law, 'I said, "You are gods"'? If He called them gods, to whom the word of God came (and the Scripture cannot be broken),"

- Jesus said to the Pharisees that this is written in your law that ye are "Elohim" to whom the Word of God has been given. It is not possible to revoke that. The Word cannot be revoked.
- The Pharisees started quivering; they got that nervousness.

❖ If the Commander sends me back to a generation and I have already died, so I am not afraid to die, then what do I have to lose if I tell you the truth? It does not matter. Paul said, "Are you now my enemy because I told you the truth?" (Galatians 4:16).

- I stared at Jesus for 45 minutes. I stared at Him so intently that I never looked down to see the nail prints in His feet.
- I never looked at His hands to see His nail prints.
- Jesus was so irresistible that I could not look away from His face, and His three feet of hair.
- I could not look away from His eyes. Inside of His eyes was a whole other world.

THE LORD IS A WARRIOR

❖ **Zephaniah 3:17** NIV "The LORD your God is with you, the Mighty Warrior who saves. He will take great delight in you; in his love he will no longer rebuke you, but will rejoice over you with singing."

- The Lord is a Warrior.
- He sings over us, and His song brings deliverance.
- He has thought of peace towards us and not of evil.
- He has an expected end for you.

In what areas of your life do you need the Lord to be a warrior? In what areas do you need the Lord to sing over you and deliver you? Take time now to pray and ask Him.

_____
_____
_____
_____

❖ **Jeremiah 29:10-12** NIV "This is what the LORD says: "When seventy years are completed for Babylon, I will come to you and fulfill my good promise to bring you back to this place. For I know the plans I have for you," declares the LORD, "plans to prosper you and not to harm you, plans to give you hope and a future. Then you will call on me and come and pray to me, and I will listen to you.

- He has plans to prosper you. Did you hear the word prosper?
- Jeremiah 29 was written before Daniel read it in exile.
- Daniel lived right before Jesus came. Daniel was taken from Israel down into Iraq, and he was exiled in Babylon.
- You ought to read the book of Daniel.

Have you doubted that God has plans to prosper you and not to harm you and plans to give you a hope and a future? Repent and call on Him, pray, and He will listen to you.

_____
_____
_____
_____

- ❖ **Daniel 9:2-3** NLT "During the first year of his reign, I, Daniel, learned from reading the word of the LORD, as revealed to Jeremiah the prophet, that Jerusalem must lie desolate for seventy years."

    - Daniel was reading the scroll of Jeremiah as a captive in Babylon, and he was reading chapter 29.
    - Daniel realized that Jeremiah was talking about him and his people in exile in Babylon.
    - He counted the years and sees that they have been in captivity for 70 years and that it was all rigged in his favor.
    - Daniel was looking at what Jeremiah wrote, years before him.
    - God said that at the end of the 70 years, they were to call on Him and pray, and God would listen to them, and bring them back to their land.
    - God said that He had plans to prosper them and give them a good end.

- Daniel saw that God said to pray, so he called a fast, and he prayed.
- Daniel knew that God was going to hear them.
- Are you surprised that an angel came to him?
- The angel said to Daniel in effect, "From the first day that you started praying, God has heard your prayer. We have been fighting to get here, but now we have come."
- They started packing, and they went back to their land, and we have Israel today.
- The Counsel of God wrapped Daniel up, took him into his future, and the angel visitation caused him to become a leader and a prophet.
- Daniel wrote all that he saw based on one thing, *the Counsel of God. He found himself in the Bible.*

Write about a time when you found *yourself* in the Bible and received the counsel of God.

_____
_____
_____
_____

- ❖ <u>**1 Corinthians 2:9-10**</u> "But as it is written: 'Eye has not seen, nor ear heard, nor have entered into the heart of man the things which God has prepared for those who love Him. But God has revealed *them* to us through His Spirit. For the Spirit searches all things, yes, the deep things of God.'"

  - What is it about you that you do not understand?
  - What is so hard about grasping the Almighty?
  - Most people end this passage at 2:9, but if you go on to 2:10, it says, "But God has revealed it to us through His Spirit."
  - You have already proved that you are limited.

- Just ask your friends, and they will tell you.
- You live in a broken world, but the Spirit is always willing.
- Jesus said, "The spirit is indeed willing, but the flesh is weak."

❖ **Romans 7:24-25** "O wretched man that I am! Who will deliver me from this body of death? I thank God—through Jesus Christ our Lord. So then, with the mind I myself serve the law of God, but with the flesh the law of sin."

❖ **Romans 8:1-2** *"There is* therefore now no condemnation to those who are in Christ Jesus, who do not walk according to the flesh, but according to the Spirit. For the law of the Spirit of life in Christ Jesus has made me free from the law of sin and death.
- Are you Romans seven or Romans eight?

CHAPTER 10

Tied up or Caught Up?

"And I know such a man—whether in the body or out of the body I do not know, God knows— how he was caught up into Paradise and heard inexpressible words, which it is not lawful for a man to utter."
2 Corinthians 12:3-4

DISCUSSION:

You need to empty yourself to make room for the new wine. What happened on the day of Pentecost? The New Testament church started this way, with a rushing mighty wind, and fire on people's heads. When was the last time that happened in the church? Utterance was next, but not just words, supernatural utterance by the Holy Spirit. In a language that the people did not know they were speaking. They were acting up to the point where Peter had to get up and apologize for the disciple's behavior. Peter, in effect, said, "I have to explain this to you because they are not drunk as you suppose. But this is that which was prophesied by the Prophet Joel. In the last days, I will pour out My Spirit on all flesh" (see Acts 2:16-17). The disciples from the upper room appeared drunk. Look how well-behaved we are now after two thousand years, we have sobered up, but that is not God's plan. You need to drink of the Spirit that Jesus spoke from. He said, "My words are Spirit, and they are life" (see John 6:63). Jesus said, "Out of your belly will come rivers of living water" (see John 7:38). Jesus showed me that water is the same water that I saw coming out from underneath the throne of our Almighty God. The River of Life runs through Heaven. I saw it fall off to the Earth, and I saw it coming up through the bellies of believers. There is plenty of river coming through you. The same fire in the altar that is before Almighty God and the same fire that is on the Seraphim's wings is in you!

When He blows on you, He is just breathing on you, but to you, it is a mighty rushing wind. We have the breath of God, and we have the fire of God, and now we have the utterance of God. The Word of God says that when we speak, we should "Speak as the very oracles of God" (see 1 Peter 4:11). We have breath, we have fire, and we have utterance. "This is that," and it has already been delivered, it is here do not wait any longer.

Are rivers of living water flowing out of your belly? If not, how can you change that?

_____
_____
_____
_____

❖ The person of the Holy Spirit cares about you. But I want to give you a press release; He actually knows more than you do. Not only that, but He has secrets.

- When I was in heaven, Jesus would whisper secrets to me.
- In Heaven, you will start on a walk, and you think that you are going to go to the end of the river of life, and well you keep walking.
- If you want to walk across the throne room? It takes almost a day, and you never want to leave.
- You will be given a chance to do something you have never done before. When you do it, you will feel so fulfilled up there that you say, "I am so glad I am home."
- Then the Lord will say, "Oh. I have something else I want to show you." It keeps going like that forever.
- Jesus will turn to His side, and you will see something about Him you have never seen before.

THE NOTES OF A WARRIOR

- **Matthew 4:4** "But He answered and said, "It is written, 'Man shall not live by bread alone, but by every word that proceeds from the mouth of God.' "

  - While we are down here, we live off every Word that comes from the Father's mouth.
  - He is the Commander of our faith.
  - God has commanded over you. He says, "You will succeed because I said you will succeed. My Word cannot be revoked.
  - The Word that I have sent out will not come back to Me void" (Isaiah 55:11).
  - We have a problem because there is a discrepancy.
  - God believes in you, but *you* do not believe in *you*.
  - You have been accepted, but do you accept yourself?
  - Why do you want to be someone else when God chose you to be who you are? You are accepted.
  - The Spirit of God says that you are adopted (see Romans 8:15). You have received the Spirit of adoption.
  - That word "adoption" means acceptance. You have the spirit of acceptance; you are loved.
  - Why are you living in Romans 7?
  - You are looking at your limitations.
  - Jesus told me that He has taken off the limitations.

You have been accepted, but do you accept *yourself*? Write out God's promise of acceptance in Romans 8:15 and stand on His Word.

_____
_____
_____
_____

- ❖ When I came back, I stopped looking at my limitations. I am running with the horses now. I met the person who made the horse, and the Lord said that what I have been faithful at, will cause me to be entrusted with greater things.

  - I learned to run with the soldiers, but I am training to run with horses.
  - It is never going to end; you will continually be receiving orders from your Commander.
  - As soon as I pass away, I will be given an ambassador's uniform.
  - I will be given authority over nations, and all the angels that are with me will be under my command, and I am the least.
  - I have already seen it, and it is all waiting for me.
  - Jesus said, "If you go back and you preach, and you teach, and you make disciples, you will rule and reign with me forever, shoulder to shoulder over nations." It is all in the Bible.

DISCUSSION:

You can find these things out by being caught up in the Counsel of your Commander. The Spirit of God is speaking to you. He is calling you out of the normal. He is calling you into the supernatural. Which means you have an attitude. "Those who love and adhere to Him, He has given them the authority to be sons of God" (John 1:12). Why is it that we skip over all the really good Scriptures? Could it be that God is too good, and you are having a hard time grasping it? I do not *skip over;* I let the Word of God transform me. The Word of God changes your mind. After your mind is changed your walk changes, and your destiny comes to you. You do not understand it because you are working really hard to get there. Jesus was standing beside me, and He took me many places that would just blow you away. The way that He took me was that the destination came to us. I did not have to move. The command was that He demanded the destination to come to us. Everything listens to Him. You thought it was just the winds and the waves that obey Him (see Matthew 8:27). You are still in that little boat, but there is more than that. The universe listens to Jesus. The water stops at the shore because He has not told it to go any further (see Psalm 33:6-10, Job 38:11). He spoke all of this into existence. He framed the worlds with His Words (see Hebrews 11:3).

If you believe God's Word, what can it do to you?
_____
_____
_____
_____

- ❖ **Mark 11:23-24** "For assuredly, I say to you, whoever says to this mountain, 'Be removed and be cast into the sea,' and does not doubt in his heart, but believes that those things he says will be done, he will have whatever he says. Therefore I say to you, whatever things you ask when you pray, believe that you receive *them,* and you will have *them.*"

    - Jesus told us that we should speak to our mountains, and if we believe in our hearts what we say with our mouths, it shall be done.
    - That was not some faith teacher that said that. That was Jesus Christ!

- ❖ **James 3:4-9** TPT "And the same with mighty ships, though they are massive and driven by fierce winds, yet they are steered by a tiny rudder at the direction of the person at the helm. And so the tongue is a small part of the body yet it carries great power! Just think of how a small flame can set a huge forest ablaze. And the tongue is a fire! It can be compared to the sum total of wickedness and is the most dangerous part of our human body. It corrupts the entire body and is a hellish flame! It releases a fire that can burn throughout the course of human existence. For every wild animal on earth including birds, creeping reptiles, and creatures of the sea and land have all been overpowered and tamed by humans, but the tongue is not able to be tamed. It's a fickle, unrestrained evil that spews out words full of toxic poison! We use our tongue to praise God our Father and then turn around and curse a person who was made in His very image!"

- James says that we have a rudder inside of our mouth like what is on a ship. It is a little thing, but it can steer a mighty ship, and it is called *your tongue*.
- Your tongue can steer your life, or it could be set on fire by the fires of hell. It says that with it, we tear down people that are made in the image of God.

❖ **Hebrews 10:12-13** "But this Man, after He had offered one sacrifice for sins forever, sat down at the right hand of God, from that time waiting till His enemies are made His footstool."

- The head of the universe is seated at the right hand of God. He is not going to do anything else until His enemies become His footstool.
- Who is going to do that? Are you one of His soldiers?
- **Warrior Note:** Soldiers have keys—keys to the Kingdom. "And I will give you the keys of the kingdom of Heaven, and whatever you bind on earth will be bound in Heaven, and whatever you loose on earth will be loosed in heaven" (John 16:19).

Jesus is in Heaven, waiting for us to make His enemies His footstool. Who are His enemies, and how do you do that?

_____
_____
_____
_____

- ❖ **John 20:23** TPT "I send you to preach the forgiveness of sins—and people's sins will be forgiven. But if you don't proclaim the forgiveness of their sins, they will remain guilty."

- ❖ **Matthew 10:14** TPT "And if anyone doesn't listen to you and rejects your message, when you leave that house or town, shake the dust off your feet *as a prophetic act that you will not take their defilement with you.*"

    - Jesus said If you forgive sins, they are forgiven.
    - He said if you go to a house and they do not treat you right, take the peace back with you.
    - He said to wipe the dust off your feet, and do not take that either.

- ❖ Jesus sent me back from glory. He sent me back from perfection to a broken world, to a broken people. People that must begin to live out of Romans chapter eight. People have to get untangled because they are tied up with the affairs of this life.

    - Jesus Himself told me, remember one thing, whatever you are going through, a thousand years from now, it is not going to matter.
    - I came from a place where you cannot lose —a place where you cannot fail. A place where you cannot think of one thing that you are afraid of — a place where you cannot doubt.
    - I came from a place where you look at Angels, and you want to have them do something for you because you know that is what they are waiting for. They want to work it. They want to bash the enemy.
    - The angels want you to give them a command that comes from the very heart of God.
    - However, you cannot do that unless you have *fire*, unless you have *counsel*, unless you have *utterance* and unless you are *drunk*.
    - You have got to be full of the Spirit, not with wine, which is excess, but be drunk in the Spirit (see Ephesians 5:18).

❖ I cannot get myself entangled with the affairs of this life, because I will be ineffective; I will cease to be effective (see 2 Timothy 2:4).

- Why don't you come to the table and dine with the Lord?
- He has set a table before you in your honor, in the presence of your enemies (Psalm 23:5). They have to stand and watch you be honored.
- Have you ever been dishonored? Well, this table honors you for it is the table of the Lord.
- The power that rests in you is the same power that rose Jesus from the dead, and it is dwelling in you (see Romans 8:11). That power is life, and it quickens your mortal body.

Jesus set a table before you in the presence of your enemies. What do you have to do to eat from that table?

_____
_____
_____
_____

❖ **Hebrews 12:22-24** "But you have come to Mount Zion and to the city of the living God, the heavenly Jerusalem, to an innumerable company of angels, to the general assembly and church of the firstborn *who are* registered in heaven, to God the Judge of all, to the spirits of just men made perfect, to Jesus the Mediator of the new covenant, and to the blood of sprinkling that speaks better things than *that of* Abel."

- The Church of the Living God—You have come to a mountain whose name is Zion, where the spirits of righteous men are made perfect.
- Are you among them? Are you among the redeemed of the Lord on the mountain of God, walking on those fiery stones?

- They are sapphire blue, as blue as the sky, with white fire going through them. I have walked on that sapphire stone.

❖ **Luke 8:26-28** "Then they sailed to the country of the Gadarenes, which is opposite Galilee. And when He stepped out on the land, there met Him a certain man from the city who had demons or a long time. And he wore no clothes, nor did he live in a house but in the tombs. When he saw Jesus, he cried out, fell down before Him, and with a loud voice said, "What have I to do with You, Jesus, Son of the Most High God? I beg You, do not torment me!"

❖ **Luke 8:30-33** "Jesus asked him, saying, "What is your name?" And he said, "Legion," because many demons had entered him. And they begged Him that He would not command them to go out into the abyss. Now a herd of many swine was feeding there on the mountain. So they begged Him that He would permit them to enter them. And He permitted them. Then the demons went out of the man and entered the swine, and the herd ran violently down the steep place into the lake and drowned."

- When Jesus got out of the boat on the other side of the lake to meet the mad man, the demons started crying out. They said, "Have you come to torment us before our time."
- The demons are nervous about torment. Thanks for letting us know!
- They do not like to be sent out of an area.
- Thanks for letting us know that as well! They are leaving your area!
- This is the Counsel of God.
- You can do this with every verse in the Bible.
- In this one passage of Scripture in the Bible, I have just shown you how much wisdom can be found there.

❖ **Warrior Note: Once you leave Romans seven and begin to live in Romans eight, you will be caught up in the Counsel of God.**

- **Mark 11:12-14** "Now the next day, when they had come out from Bethany, He was hungry. And seeing from afar a fig tree having leaves, He went to see if perhaps He would find something on it. When He came to it, He found nothing but leaves, for it was not the season for figs. In response Jesus said to it, "Let no one eat fruit from you ever again."

  - Everybody wants to know what Jesus had against the fig tree. I asked Him, "Were you in a bad mood that day?"
  - Then Jesus asked me, "What if you had eaten from the fruit that I told you not to, and you fell, and your eyes were opened? Then what if you saw that you were naked, and you grabbed the nearest thing to cover yourself?"
  - Who said it was an apple, it is not in the Bible?
  - Jesus told me, "I hate religion." He said, "The fig tree was man's way of dealing with sin, covering it up. My way of dealing with it is blood. I cursed that system that man chose, and I cursed that tree because I remembered it as I walked by it. Man's solution to sin does not work."
  - Do you think those animals just unzipped their fur and handed it to God to give to Adam and Eve? No, they died…they shed their blood.
  - Those animals lost their life because God said, "No, it's not going to be the fig tree. It is going to be blood."
  - Jesus explained to me that God set the way. It was going to be blood.
  - When Jesus walked by that fig tree that had no fruit, it reminded Him of man's way.
  - The Word of God says, "By their fruit you will know them" (see Romans 7:16).
  - You do not have any fruit living in Romans, chapter 7.

THE NOTES OF A WARRIOR

What area of your life has the accuser of the brethren been tormenting you? Take your authority and cast him out in Jesus' name. Jesus' blood was enough; you are forgiven.

_____

_____

_____

_____

- ❖ Are you tied up or caught up? Is Jesus' blood enough. Have you messed up too much that there is still something exposed? No. The blood was enough. There is no accusing voice against you because you are forgiven. I will prove it to you.

- ❖ <u>Isaiah 1:18</u> "Come now, and let us reason together," Says the LORD, "Though your sins are like scarlet, they shall be as white as snow; Though they are red like crimson, they shall be as wool."

    - He said that I am going to wash away your sins, and they are going to be white, even though they were crimson.
    - He is going to wipe them out—completely wipe them out.
    - When I was in Heaven, Jesus did not know that I had ever sinned! I thought, no, but then, He cannot be lying, because I was looking right into His eyes. He was talking to me as though I had never sinned.
    - I looked into His eyes, and He did know that I had sinned. He does not have access to the file of my past or your past. It was not available because it was destroyed.
    - You have got to accept that.
    - <u>**Warrior Note**</u>**: A good soldier does not have a past; He has a future.**
    - A soldier does not stare at his trophies in his office because he is out making more; he is obtaining more awards.

149

- You want to know why? It is because he can, and he does not take no for an answer. These are the personality traits of a soldier.
- So, are you tied up or caught up?
- If you are a good soldier, you are hearing your Commander's voice.
- You have been hearing the Commander speaking to you through this Study Guide.

❖ Did you know that Ministry is not a job? Did you know that Ministry does not exist on this earth; it comes from Heaven.

- My relationship is my ministry. I do not have a job.
- I have a calling, and I am chosen.
- You are chosen and the callings and gifts of God are irrevocable according to Scripture (see Romans 11:29).
- You need to be fully convinced of your Commander. He is fully convinced of you, or He would not have chosen you.

❖ Jesus said this to me, "If all we were supposed to do is get born again, and then just wait for Him to come back, then why didn't I just take you at the altar when you gave your life to the Lord?"

Since Jesus did not take you home when you became born again, then what are you doing here? What is stopping you from being in the will of God?

_____
_____
_____
_____

- ❖ **2 Thessalonians 2:7-8** "For the mystery of lawlessness is already at work; only He who now restrains *will do so* until He is taken out of the way. And then the lawless one will be revealed, whom the Lord will consume with the breath of His mouth and destroy with the brightness of His coming."

  - Paul said in Thessalonians that the antichrist would not appear until he who is holding him back is taken out. We are the ones that are keeping him back.
  - The Bride of Christ is on the earth. Jesus is coming back to take the bride with Him. As long as you are on duty, the devil is a victim.
  - You are *not* the victim.

- ❖ **2 Timothy 1:12** "For this reason I also suffer these things; nevertheless I am not ashamed, for I know whom I have believed and am persuaded that He is able to keep what I have committed to Him until that Day."

  - Paul said that he was fully convinced, and we can be as well. I know who I have believed in. I am fully persuaded that He is able to take hold and keep that which I have committed unto Him until that day.

- ❖ **Philippians 3:12** "Not that I have already attained, or am already perfected; but I press on, that I may lay hold of that for which Christ Jesus has also laid hold of me."

  - We need to take hold of that, which He has taken hold for you. Paul was holding on to Christ, and He is extending His hand to you as well.
  - The Apostle Paul was caught up, as you know. He said he could not tell you everything, but he would tell you what he could. He said that he saw things that he could not even repeat (see 2 Corinthians 12:4).

- **Ephesians 3:20** "Now to Him who is able to do exceedingly abundantly above all that we ask or think, according to the power that works in us,"

  - Think of the best thing that God can do for you, and He is going to do even more than that.
  - Our perception has to change. When we say, "God, You can do this." God says, "I can do better than that. Forever, abundantly and above what you could ask or think."
  - Our vantage point from where we stand has to change.

- Jesus spoke to John who got caught up on the Isle of Patmos, "Tell the churches that he who overcomes and is victorious shall sit with Me on a throne" (see Revelation 3:21).

  - What is this other throne? Come up and be seated. "And raised us up together and made us sit together in the Heavenly realms in Christ Jesus" (see Ephesians 2:6).
  - You are seated with Him in the Heavenly realms. It's not that you are going to be, but that you already are!
  - This is eternity. This is your life.
  - The next breath that comes out of Jesus is your next inhale. He breathes out, and you breathe in.

Where are you seated with Christ Jesus? Get caught up!

_____
_____
_____
_____

THE NOTES OF A WARRIOR

- ❖ **Matthew 7:13-14** "Enter by the narrow gate; for wide *is* the gate and broad *is* the way that leads to destruction, and there are many who go in by it. Because narrow *is* the gate and difficult *is* the way which leads to life, and there are few who find it."

    - Do not be like Judas. Do not find yourself on the wrong side. There is a narrow way, and few find it. Wide is the way to destruction, and many go there.
    - Jesus said that the narrow way is the way.

- ❖ **John 14:6** "Jesus said to him, "I am the way, the truth, and the life. No one comes to the Father except through Me."

- ❖ **John 10:9** "I am the door. If anyone enters by Me, he will be saved, and will go in and out and find pasture."

    - Jesus said, "I am the door. No one comes to the Father except through Me." No religious leader has the right or the authority to say there are many ways to God.
    - Jesus Christ said there is one way. He said He was the door.
    - He is the truth, and He is the life.

DISCUSSION:

I don't know about you, but I am enlisted in the best army, and I have the best soldiers by my side. There is victory in the power of the Holy Spirit. "No weapon formed against you shall prosper" (see Isaiah 54:17). This Scripture is not just a positive confession because absolute truth originated from Heaven. Paul said, "The Word of God did not originate with man, but holy men of old were breathed on and moved by the Holy Ghost and wrote" (see 2 Peter 1:21). That is where the Word of God came from; the other realm. I am telling you the truth. The angels come because they are believing that you will actually engage in combat. See *yourself* in the Word of God and know that it is all rigged in your favor!

"There is nothing that can stop you from obeying God. I have cleared the way for you." says the Lord. "I have destroyed what is before you. I have come with fire, and I burn the enemy. I chase him out. Holy Fire. The angels have come to engage."

The Angel of the Lord came to Joshua. Joshua said, "Are you for us or against us?" The angel said, "Neither, but as the Angel of the Lord, I have come" (see Joshua 5:13-14). He was sent. He was not entangled in your drama. Angels are soldiers that are caught up in the Counsel of God. If you ask them if they are in your mess or not in your mess, they are going to say, "No, as the Angel of the Lord we have come." The Angels of God only know victory, and they only know that you need to be caught up.

The Spirit of God is a Commander of the blessing. He is an Enforcer of the blessing. The Spirit of God does not curse you. "Jesus with the Holy Spirit went around doing good and healing everyone that was oppressed of the devil, for God was with Him" (see Acts 10:38). He only did what His Father told Him to do. "Surely goodness and mercy shall follow me all the days of my life (Psalm 23:6). Give the Lord permission to command you today and every day!

About Dr. Kevin Zadai

Kevin Zadai was called to ministry at the age of ten. He attended Central Bible College in Springfield, Missouri, where he received a Bachelor of Arts in Theology. Later, he received training in missions at Rhema Bible College. He is currently ordained through Rev. Dr. Jesse and Rev. Dr. Cathy Duplantis. At age thirty-one, during a routine day surgery, he found himself on the "other side of the veil" with Jesus. For forty-five minutes, the Master revealed spiritual truths before returning him to his body and assigning him to a supernatural ministry. Kevin holds a commercial pilot license and has been employed by Southwest Airlines for twenty-nine years as a flight attendant. He and his lovely wife, Kathi, reside in New Orleans, Louisiana.

DR. KEVIN L. ZADAI

Salvation Prayer

Lord God,

I confess that I am a sinner. I confess that I need Your Son, Jesus. Please forgive me in His name.

Lord Jesus, I believe You died for me and that You are alive and listening to me now.

I now turn from my sins and welcome You into my heart. Come and take control of my life. Make me the kind of person You want me to be.

Now, fill me with Your Holy Spirit who will show me how to live for You. I acknowledge You before men as my Savior and my Lord.

In Jesus's name. Amen.

If you prayed this prayer, please contact us at: info@kevinzadai.com for more information and material. Go to kevinzadai.com for other exciting ministry materials.

Kevinzadai.com

To enroll in our ministry school, go to:

Warriornotesschool.com

God's Six days of Creation

In the beginning God created the heavens and the earth. Now the earth was formless and empty, darkness was over the surface of the deep. And the Spirit of God was hovering over the waters.

Genesis 1:1-2

502727 8754

Lola's Lion
By Samaritans Purse, ORG